# hide
# this
# french
# book

Apa Publications GmbH and Co. Verlag KG

New York          Munich          Singapore

Contacting the Editors
Every effort has been made to provide accurate information in this publication, but changes are inevitable. The publisher cannot be responsible for any resulting loss, inconvenience or injury. We would appreciate it if readers would call our attention to any errors or outdated information; please contact us: Apa Publications, 193 Morris Avenue, Springfield, NJ 07081, USA. E-mail: hidethisxtreme@langenscheidt.com

First Printing: December 2009
Printed in Singapore

Publishing Director: Sheryl Olinsky Borg
Senior Editor/Project Manager: Lorraine Sova
Writer: Brian Jacobs
Reviewer: Marie Ollivier-Caudray
Interior Design: Wee Design Group
Composition: Datagrafix, Inc.
Cover Design: Claudia Petrilli
Illustrator: Tatiana Davidova
Production Manager: Elizabeth Gaynor
Interior Photos: page 10 © 2009 Jupiterimages Corporation; page 87 © Kermarrec Aurelien, Used under license from istockphoto.com; © Effinity Stock Photography, Used under license from istockphoto.com; ©ShyMan, Used under license from istockphoto.com; © Brett Charlton, Used under license from istockphoto.com; © Parema, Used under license from istockphoto.com

# INSIDE

# INTRO

Which would you say or text to your BFF?

a. Hello, would you like to attend a party tonight?
b. Hey dude/bitch, wanna hang out 2nite?

If you picked option a, close this book now (we're warning you!). But, if you picked b, keep on reading…

This book is *not* for people who want to sound like they just got off the plane when they visit France. It should be used only by cool people who want to learn how to speak *real* French. There are no verb conjugations, no grammar lessons and no rules with all kinds of exceptions. The language included in this book is what the young, hip French really speak today—and we've made it as easy as possible for you pick up and use. You'll navigate your way through everything from dating and sex to fashion and style.

## WHAT YOU NEED TO KNOW

We're assuming that you may already know a little French, but it's OK if you don't. The expressions included in this book are translated with their closest equivalent in English—there isn't always a direct translation. We explain everything you need to know, and you can even hear some of the expressions in this book at our website, www.langenscheidt.com/hidethis. Look for: 🔊 . So, you don't only know *what* to say, but *how* to say it!

You may just want to listen to them with headphones so you don't offend anyone…

## SEX

Got your attention? Words or expressions followed by ♂ are for guys only and those with ♀ are for girls only.

## BOMBS AWAY!

We've labeled the really bad stuff clearly to try and save you from some uncomfortable situations. Here's how it works:

💣* means that you can use these words around your friends and sound cool;
💣*💣* are used for words that are completely inappropriate, incredibly offensive and downright dirty! You should use these words only with your closest friends and definitely *not* around French old folks, teachers, etc.

# FEATURES

You'll also notice these different features throughout the book:

**Manga** Cool comics that feature cool French language

**Dialogue** Conversations between French hipsters

**Word Bytes** A list of key words from the manga or dialogue

**All That Slang** Short sentences, phrases or words for lots of crazy situations

**A-List** The best of the best—the shortlist of the hottest things

**Use It or Lose It!** Fun activities that get you using the slanguage you've picked up

**Quiz** Interactive quizzes that test your personality and knowledge of French slang

**Mixed Up** A French-English game that lets you LOL while practicing your French

**Q&A** Our very own cultural and language advice column

For when you want to be naughty or nice

**Know-it-all/Tout savoir** Interesting facts on French slang and culture, from our resident nerd named Tout savoir, which means "know-it-all" in French

**Gestures** How to say it—visually

## AND LAST BUT NOT LEAST...

Languages are constantly evolving—what's in today might be out tomorrow—and while we've done our best to give you the coolest and most up-to-date slang, it's possible that some of the expressions might go out of fashion. So, if you come across anything in this book that's outdated or if you learn a cool new expression that you think we should include in the future, we'd love to hear from you! Send us an e-mail at: hidethisxtreme@langenscheidt.com.

# Get info on:

- different ways to say cool
- how to say something sucks

## 🔊 That's cool!

 **Know-it-all/Tout savoir**

*"Cool" or "cold"—as in temperature—in French is **froid**.
Don't use this literal translation to mean "cool" as above.
Be careful: If you say that a woman is **froide**, it can mean
that she's frigid and that can be very not cool!*

# ◉ All That Slang

Although you can say *cool* in French, but why not mix it up a little? Here are some other, more authentic, words you can use.

| | |
|---|---|
| **Génial !** | **Trop fort !** |
| **Excellent !** | **Ça déchire !** |
| **Super !** | **Ça pète !** |
| **Top !** | **C'est de la balle !** |

# A-List

Now that you know some different ways to say cool, let's see what's considered cool in France and other French-speaking countries.

**petite voiture**          compact car

*L'essence* (gas) has always cost *la peau des fesses* (a hell of a lot, literally, the skin of the butt) in France. So, the French tend to shy away from gas-guzzling SUVs and stick to smaller, more environmentally-friendly cars.

**la bande dessinée, la BD**   comic book

Comic books are so cool that when you go into a *librairie*, a bookstore, you can sometimes find an entire floor dedicated to them!

**parfum**          perfume/cologne

The French are known the world over for creating some fantastic fragrances!

# Use It or Lose It!

To express coolness, use these phrases. Just add the cool word of choice.

C'est _____ !

C'est grave _____ !

C'est trop _____ !

*C'est trop cool !*
That's really cool!

*Génial !*
Awesome!

*Ça déchire !*
This is fucking great!

*Putain, c'est trop fort !*
How fucking cool!

# Q&A

**Chère Virginie:**

Last month I went to my cousin's house in Lyon. We were talking about Madonna's latest video and how Brigitte Bardot would never approve of the leather pants she wears in it. My cousin kept repeating over and over again "That video *pète sa mère*". I don't understand what he meant, since *péter* means to explode or to fart and *mère* means mother. I don't get it. Is there something wrong with his mother?!

Sincerely,
Troublé (Confused)

**Cher Troublé:**

No need for alarm—nobody is going to explode! *Ça pète sa mère* is an expression that young people use to say something is "too cool" or "off the hook". So, learn the phrase and use it!

À bientôt !
Virginie

**Chère Virginie:**

The other day, a French-speaking classmate told me that my presentation was *de la bombe*. Is he trying to tell me that I bombed my presentation and that it sucked or am I just overreacting? What does it really mean?

Yours,
Offensée (Offended)

**Chère Offensée:**

He was just paying you a compliment on your cool presentation! *De la bombe* means bomb, which also means great or awesome in French slang, just like in English.

À bientôt !
Virginie

## Know-it-all/Tout savoir

The expression "to keep one's cool" can be translated as **garder son sang-froid/rester calme.**

9

# Dialogue: Jean et Kate

Jean spots Kate, an exchange student, at the bar. He's trying to start a conversation by telling her she looks cool. He obviously likes her. But Kate doesn't understand...

| | | |
|---|---|---|
| JEAN: | **Salut, Kate !** | Hello, Kate! |
| KATE: | **Salut, Jean !** | Hello, Jean! |
| JEAN: | **T'as l'air énorme ce soir !** | You're looking *énorme* this evening! |
| KATE: | **ÉNORME ?** (she slaps him) | *ÉNORME?* |
| JEAN: | **Attends... Kate... Énorme veut dire cool.** | Wait...Kate... *Énorme* means cool. |
| KATE: | **Oops, désolée... je me suis trompée.** | Oops, sorry... my bad. |
| JEAN: | (to himself) **Quelle gifle...** | What a slap... |

What do you think Kate understood?

# Use It or Lose It!

How would you say cool if you were...?

1. in class
2. with your friends
3. a potty mouth
4. in any situation

1. super, sympa, génial; 2. ça déchire; 3. ça pète; 4. cool—remember you can never go wrong with cool, said with a French accent, of course

# 🔊 That's un-cool!

# 🔊 All That Slang

For every cool thing there is an un-cool thing. Here's how to say something sucks.

| | |
|---|---|
| **C'est nul.** | It's worthless. |
| **C'est merdique./C'est de la merde.** | It's shitty. *You can also say any noun (car, work, person, etc.) **merdique** or **de merde**. For example, **Quelle voiture de merde!** means What a shitty car!* |
| **C'est pourri.** | It's garbage. *Literally, It's rotten/spoiled.* |
| **C'est con.** 💣 | That's stupid. **Con** *can mean pussy, and we're not talking about the cat!* |
| **C'est dég/dégueulasse.** 💣 | That's gross. *From the French word* **dégueuler**, *which means to throw up.* |
| **Putain, c'est nul à chier!** 💣💣 | It fucking sucks! *Literally, Whore, it's worthless to the point of shitting!* |

11

*There is no concrete word to say that something sucks in French, but one thing is sure: you'll never hear someone say **ça suce**, literally, it sucks, because that has a WHOLE different connotation. So get your mind out of the gutter and practice the many other ways to say something sucks!*

# Use It or Lose It!

What's the right response for each situation? Don't mess up! (No pressure…)

a. Your best friend is showing off a brand-new MP3 player with voice recognition.

b. Your 67-year-old grandmother has been asked if she is pregnant by a 4-year-old.

c. Your best friend got you tickets to see your favorite band.

d. Your cousin slapped an old lady's ass.

e. Your friend has just been promoted.

1. **C'est génial !**
2. **C'est dég !**
3. **Ça pète !**
4. **C'est trop fort !**
5. **C'est nul !**

1. e; 2. d; 3. c; 4. a; 5. b

# Word Bytes

You're gonna need to know these for the quiz on the next page!

| | | | |
|---|---|---|---|
| **à la maison** | at home | **l'invitation** | invitation |
| **l'ami ♂/l'amie ♀** | friend | **le marathon** | marathon |
| **la chemise** | shirt | **merci** | thanks |
| **chouette** | neat, nifty | **n'importe quoi** | anything |
| **le coin** | corner | **la plage** | beach |
| **le dimanche** | Sunday | **tata** | auntie |
| **la famille** | family | | |

1. If invited to *une fête* you:
   a. check your calendar—you have *beaucoup d'invitations*!
   b. say *merci*, and then go home to watch a *film* with close *amis*.
   c. go, sit in *le coin*, then wonder why you went.

2. Your cell phone contact list has:
   a. so many people—including all the *amis* you made on spring break in the French Riviera—you don't remember half of them.
   b. good *amis*, *famille* and the Chinese delivery phone number.
   c. your mom, grandma and *tata* on speed dial.

3. Your favorite outfit is:
   a. whatever's in style now—and it always looks *classe* on you.
   b. classic, like *un jean* and *une chemise*. You always look clean.
   c. whatever you have on hand: jogging pants and *un sweat*, a sweatshirt. *N'importe quoi*.

4. Your favorite French expression for cool is:
   a. *Putain, ça pète sa mère !* 💣 💣
   b. *Trop fort* or *Génial*.
   c. *Chouette*.

5. *Le dimanche*, you'd rather:
   a. wake up and continue *la fête*.
   b. go to *la plage*, catch a *film* or enjoy a relaxing day *à la maison* on your own.
   c. enjoy *un marathon de films* of your choice with some of your *amis*.

**Mainly As: *ça pète***
You are so *cool* you're hot. But careful, some people might think you're too cool to be true!

**Mainly Bs: *super-cool***
You may not be the life of the party, but you don't care and that makes you *génial*.

**Mainly Cs: *chouette***
Don't try to be *super*—enjoy yourself and others will enjoy spending time with you too. You are *excellent*♂/*excellente*♀ in your own way.

# Use It or Lose It!

Off the top of your head—without looking back—name 10 cool and/or un-cool words you now know in French. Write down your answers, then try reading your answers aloud in front of a mirror to see how *super* (or un-*super*) you look.

# Friends & Family

## chapter 2

## Get info on:

- nicknames and pet names
- meeting people and talking with friends
- slang about family members

## All That Slang

Terms for strangers, acquaintances, friends and lovers…

**type, mec, keum\* ♂ / nana, meuf\* ♀**

*\*Keum and meuf are in verlan, a kind of French slang. See the Know-it-all/Tout savoir on the next page to learn how the French create and use verlan.*

guy/girl

**beau gosse ♂ / super nana ♀**

a hottie

**connard 💣☀**

asshole

**chum (Canada), pote**

buddy

**snob**
snob

**richard**
richie
*a term
reserved for
wealthy people*

**vieille fille ♀**
old fart, spinster
*literally, old girl*

**pauvre naze**
dumbass

**fêtard ♂/fêtarde ♀**
party animal

### Know-it-all/Tout savoir

*French hipsters from Parisian suburbs started* **verlan**—*a kind of French slang—to confuse the uncool.* **Verlan** *works by rearranging the order of letters or syllables in a word. You take the last letter or syllable of a word and move it to the front. For example,* **femme** *(woman) becomes* **meuf**, **flic** *(cop) becomes* **keuf** *and* **branché** *(trendy) becomes* **chébran**. *Keep your eyes peeled throughout the book for more examples of* **verlan**.

15

# Use It or Lose It!

Can you find these people in this party scene?

- **pote**
- **vieille fille**
- **super nana**
- **fêtard**

## Word Bytes

You gotta know these to take the quiz…

| | | | |
|---|---|---|---|
| **l'alcool** | alcohol | **la famille** | family |
| **beaucoup de** | a lot, much | **la fête** | party |
| **le café** | coffee | **mémé** | grandma |
| **la danse** | dance | **la musique** | music |
| **la personnalité** | personality | **sympa** | nice |
| **le copain/la copine** | boyfriend/girlfriend | **le vin rouge** | red wine |

Are you a *snob*, *mec* ♂ /*nana* ♀ *sympa* or *fêtard* ♂ / *fêtarde* ♀ ? Find out.

**1.** You're enjoying your day at the beach on the Côte d'Azur by:
   **a.** covering up with SPF 70 and an oversized T-shirt.
   **b.** playing beach volleyball with the *mecs et nanas* next to you. After the game, you and your new friends have a few drinks to celebrate.
   **c.** finding the perfect spot on one of the many topless beaches, then asking a *beau gosse* or a *super nana* to rub oil on your back.

**2.** At *la fête de la famille*:
   **a.** your *mémé* slips you some money for being so nice—you baked dessert and offered to drive your drunk aunt home.
   **b.** you bring some *vin rouge*, jump around with the *gamins* (kids) and leave early to meet your friends.
   **c.** you don't show up; you're tired of the family yapping about how you should get off your ass and do something with your life.

**3.** *La fête* is:
   **a.** a dinner party with your close friends, which you and your *copain* ♂ / *copine* ♀ lovingly prepared together.
   **b.** getting together with friends, where the conversation is as important as the food and drinks!
   **c.** any place with *de la musique, de la danse* and *beaucoup d'alcool…*

**4.** *La fête* ends at:
   **a.** 10 o'clock, sharp—you need your eight hours (or more) of beauty sleep.
   **b.** 10, 11, 12, 1—it depends on the *fête…*
   **c.** never!

**Mainly As:** *snob*
You want to be perfect and often forget to have fun. People in the office rarely talk to you; they're afraid you will backstab them to get points with the boss. Still, you have a few good friends who really care about you. You won't get skin cancer, but you probably have an ulcer the size of France.

**Mainly Bs:** *mec sympa* ♂ /*nana sympa* ♀
You are the life of the *fête*; everybody likes you! When you're not there, people notice. Keep it up and have fun—you only live once!

**Mainly Cs:** *fêtard* ♂ /*fêtarde* ♀
You're too extreme. Still there is some hope if you reel it in a little. Also, consider getting strangers to rub some SPF 60 on your back instead of tanning oil.

# All That Slang

When you're on a first name basis with French speakers, try out some nicknames. Here are some of the most popular.

| NAME | NICKNAME |
|------|----------|
| Alexandre | Alex |
| Benoît | Ben |
| Florent/Florence | Flo |
| Frédéric/Frédérique | Fred |
| Grégoire | Greg |
| Jean-Jacques | JJ *pronounced zsee-zsee (the zs is like Zsa Zsa)* |
| Jean-Paul | JP *pronounced zsee-pay* |
| Laurent/Laurence | Lolo |
| Pierre | Pierrot |
| Sophie | Soso |
| Véronique | Véro |
| Virginie | Vivi |

Nicknames are often used as a way of expressing affection in French.

# Use It or Lose It!

What are these people's real names?

Lolo    Vivi    Flo    Soso    Alex    Pierrot    JP    JJ

# All That Slang

In case you forget someone's name, avoid embarrassment by using a pet name. Note: You'd be surprised how much people use pet names in French, so don't be afraid to give it a try! You can also use these with your close friends and family.

| | | | |
|---|---|---|---|
| bébé | baby | ma belle ♀ | my beauty |
| chéri ♂/chérie ♀ | darling | ma biche ♀, ma bibiche ♀ | my doe |
| chouchou | honey | mon trésor | my treasure |
| mon amour | my love | ma puce | my sweetie |

# Q&A

**Chère Vivi:**

I went to Paris last summer. I heard before I left that the French can be quite *snob* with foreigners and that I wouldn't make any friends. I was afraid to talk to anyone at first, but after just a few days I realized that there are so many nice people there! They helped me practice my French and I helped them with their English—it was a great exchange. So, does the fact that I find them *super cool* mean that I am *snob* too or are the French really just nice people in general?

Merci mille fois !
Jack

**Cher Jack:**

People in Paris are warm and inviting (of course there are exceptions), and they enjoy chatting with foreigners—after all, Paris is the most visited city in the whole world. You just have to be nice to them too. Don't walk up to someone on the street in Paris and assume he or she speaks English. Opening with *Parlez-vous anglais ?* can make a world of difference.

Bien à toi,
Vivi

**Chère Vivi:**

When I first met my friend, Bruno, from France, he gave me two kisses, one on each cheek. I found it weird, but I was also happy, because he's so cute and I figured it meant he obviously likes me... I think. It turns out he's happily married, though. When I met his wife, she gave me three kisses: two on one cheek and one on the other. I haven't invited them to my house yet—I'm afraid they want a *ménage à trois*. What should I do?!?

Effrayée (Scared),
Jane

**Chère Jane:**

Don't be *conne*. It's customary for the French to kiss friends and family (and even strangers) as a greeting. Your friend's wife is most likely from the south of France, where three kisses are alternated from cheek to cheek (and after all these years I still never know which cheek to start with!). You won't be expected to kiss anyone but, when someone kisses you, take it with grace, even if it's someone you're meeting for the first time. Drop your guard and pucker up (and don't be too quick to call your harassment lawyer).

Bises,
Vivi

# Use It or Lose It!

Finish this message using pet names.

_____ (my love), I just wanted to tell you that Pierre and I have decided to be together. Pierre is _____ (my baby). Sorry, _____ (my treasure), remember that you will always be my _____ (darling), _____ (honey).

Mon amour; mon bébé; mon trésor; chéri; chouchou

# Dialogue: Les potins

Wanna gossip like the *commères* in this conversation?

| | | |
|---|---|---|
| ROBERT: | **On te l'a dit ?** | Did anybody tell you? |
| CHRISTINE: | **Quoi ?** | What? |
| ROBERT: | **Le voisin du dessous a un nouveau copain…** | The guy from the apartment below has a new boyfriend… |
| CHRISTINE: | **Ah bon ? Comment ça ?** | Really? How so? |
| ROBERT: | **Oui, c'est Hélène qui me l'a dit. Tu ne devineras jamais qui c'est…** | Yes, Hélène told me. You'll never guess who it is… |
| CHRISTINE: | **C'est qui ?** | Who? |
| ROBERT: | **Le frère de son ex-copine !** | His ex-girlfriend's brother! |
| CHRISTINE: | **Putain, j'y crois pas. 💣✳** | Holy shit, I can't believe it. |
| ROBERT: | **Quel bordel !** | What a mess! |

# Word Bytes

| | |
|---|---|
| **cancaner** | to gossip |
| **la commère** | a gossip (person) |
| **l'histoire** ♀ | story |
| **mentir** | lie |
| **les potins** | gossip (info) |
| **quoi** | what |
| **le voisin** ♂ **/la voisine** ♀ | neighbor |

# Use It or Lose It!

Can you pass the polygraph? Write *vrai* if the statement from the *potin* is true, or *faux* if it's not.

1. In the beginning, Christine does not believe what Robert is telling her.
2. Christine told Robert the *rumeur*.
3. The dude downstairs is dating someone new.

1. vrai; 2. faux, Hélène told the rumeur to Robert, and he told Christine; 3. vrai

# All That Slang

If you want to know more than you should, you gotta learn to gossip! Memorize these phrases to get what you want.

| | |
|---|---|
| **Qu'est-ce qui s'est passé ?** | What happened? |
| **Quel bordel !** | What a mess! |
| **T'es au courant ?** | Did you hear? |
| **On m'a dit que...** | They told me that... |
| **Je ne savais pas.** | I didn't know. |
| **J'ai entendu dire que...** | I heard that... |
| **Qui te l'a dit ?** | Who told you? |

## Know-it-all/Tout savoir

To know more about **les potins**, check out French magazines like **Public**, **Voici** and **Paris-Match**. These are some of the many magazines that follow the lives of French people's favorite celebrities. Read these and learn how to gossip like a pro—in French!

# Use It or Lose It!

Finish this juicy bit of gossip.

JEAN-PAUL: Cécile, _____? (Did you hear?)

CÉCILE: _____? (What happened?)

JEAN-PAUL: Le truc sur Michel... (The thing about Michel...)

CÉCILE: _____ . (No.)

JEAN-PAUL: Il a détruit la voiture du voisin. (He wrecked the neighbor's car.)

CÉCILE: _____ (What a mess!)

¡ T'es au courant ?; De quoi ?; Non.; Quel bordel !

## Gestures

This gesture has a few different meanings in French. Put your hands up, raise your eyebrows, pucker your lips and say one of the following:

**C'est pas de ma faute !**
It's not my fault!

**Je n'en sais rien, moi !**
I don't know anything about it!

If your friend is a bit too much of a _fêtard♂ / fêtarde♀_ and is _bourré♂ / bourrée♀ de chez bourré♂ / bourrée♀_ (drunk off his/her ass), use this gesture to show just how drunk he/she is!

_Mon œil !_ Yeah right! If your friend is telling you a far-fetched story that you don't believe for a second, give him or her this gesture to show that you're not believing a word of it.

# 🔊 Guillaume's dysfunctional family

Quoi ?!
What!?

**mémé cool (tatouée)**
cool (tattooed) grandma

Aïe !
Ouch!

**pépé a mal partout**
achy grandpa

Je prends soin de ma famille.
I take care of my family.

**maman vieux jeu**
old-fashioned mom

Où sont mes lunettes ?
Where are my glasses?

**papa distrait**
forgetful father

Je tiens de ma mère.
I take after my mom.

**oncle rocker**
rocker uncle

J'adore ma famille.
I love my family.

**tante ridicule**
ridiculous aunt

Je ne me suis jamais mariée.
I've never been married.

**tante vieille fille**
spinster aunt

Ma famille est géniale !
My family is awesome!

**Guillaume (Guy)**
William (Bill)

JE VEUX MA MAMAN !
I want my mommy!

**frère geignard**
whiny brother

Je ne supporte pas ma famille.
I can't stand my family.

**cousine qui se la pète**
arrogant cousin

Fous-moi la paix !
Leave me the hell alone!

**cousine gothique**
goth cousin

# Mixed Up

Try this grown-up version of fill-in-the-blank…

a. name for goth sister
c. name for arrogant brother
b. name for hottie ♂
d. name for mindless mom

Laure, the _____ is waiting for her date to arrive. The doorbell rings.
a

A _____ is at the door. Laure gets up to greet him, but is intercepted
b

by _____. Philippe, the _____, and the _____
c                                    c                                    b

know each other! Then, the _____ walks in and says to her
d

daughter, "I thought *you* had a date?!"

# 🔊 All That Slang

Expand your slanguage on family members…

| | |
|---|---|
| **gosse, gamin** ♂ **/gamine** ♀ | kid |
| **pater** ♂ **/mater** ♀ | old man/old lady<br>*Use these to talk about your parents.* |
| **papa** ♂ **/maman** ♀ | daddy/mommy |
| **mari** ♂ **/femme** ♀ | husband/wife |
| **pépé** ♂ **/mémé** ♀ | grandpa/grandma *You may also hear*<br>***papy*** *and* ***mamy***. |
| **tonton** | uncle |
| **tata, tati** | auntie |
| **frangin** ♂ **/frangine** ♀ | brother/sister |

# Use It or Lose It!

Can you ID everyone in this family picture?

1. _____

2. _____

3. _____

4. _____

5. _____

6. _____

1. frangine; 2. papa; 3. maman; 4. frangin; 5. mémé or mamy; 6. pépé or papy

### Know-it-all/Tout savoir

Godparents are still very important in many French families. Originally the **parrain** (godfather) and **marraine** (godmother) were meant to help the parents in the religious education of the child, but nowadays they're usually just the ones who give the best presents on holidays!

**Chère Vivi:**

My French friend Sylvain invited me to his house the other day for dinner. I met his *parents*\*, his *frangin* and even his *grands-parents*\*. I practiced my French with them and addressed everybody as *tu* (you), but after the dinner Sylvain told me that I was a little rude to his family. What gives?

> Troublée,
> Jane

\*You can just say *parents* and *grands-parents* in French too— pretty sweet, huh? Just don't forget to use a French accent!

**Chère Jane:**

Be careful which form of "you" you use to address people you don't know well in France. It's perfectly fine to use *tu* (you, informal) with Sylvain's *frangin*, but you should really use *vous* (you, formal) when addressing his *parents* and especially his *grand-mère* and *grand-père*.

Note: In French-speaking Canada they're much more relaxed about the use of *tu* and *vous*, so don't be surprised if some random guy on the street uses the *tu* form with you. It's cool in Canada!

> Vivi

**Chère Vivi:**

I've been invited to the neighbors' *mariage* (wedding) in Bordeaux and they told me that it's going to be an all-night party. They don't seem like big *fêtards*, though, so what's the deal?

> Curieux,
> George

**Cher George:**

A *mariage* in France isn't quite like your typical wedding elsewhere. Sure, there's a beautiful wedding gown, a cake, music and dancing, but the French like to party all night long. A normal wedding in France can start in the early evening and last until 2 or 3 o'clock in the morning. There's singing, there's dancing and there's usually quite a lot to drink. And yes, even *mémé* and *pépé* stick around until the end!

> Vivi

# Gay & Lesbian

## chapter 3

## Get info on:

- the usual and not so usual terms for "gay"
- gay-friendly phrases

## 🔊 All That Slang

Warning! These terms are insulting when used inappropriately.

♂ ♂ How to say "gay"…

| | |
|---|---|
| **un gay** | **une pédale** 💣 |
| **un homo** | **une tapette** 💣 |
| **un pédé** 💣 | **une tarlouze** 💣 |

♀ ♀ How to say "lesbian"…

**une lesbienne** 💣

**une gouine** 💣

**une goudou** 💣

**une broute-gazon** 💣

♂ ♀ different gender-benders…

| | |
|---|---|
| **une drag-queen** | drag queen |
| **un transsexuel** ♂ / **une transsexuelle** ♀ | transsexual |
| **un travesti** ♂ /**une travestie** ♀ | transvestite |

### Know-it-all/Tout savoir

*Be PC and use these terms: **gay/lesbienne, bi, transsexuel** ♂/**transsexuelle** ♀, **travesti** ♂/**travestie** ♀. No English translations needed, right?! All other terms can be highly offensive, except when used by those in the LGBT community.*

# Use It or Lose It!

Identify each by their slang name.

1.

2.

3.

4.

1. gouine; 2. bi; 3. travesti; 4. gay

 **Know-it-all/Tout savoir**

Paris is not only the cultural capital of France, it's also the gay capital. If you're asking yourself "Where're the gays at?" head on over to the **Marais** in the historic 4th Arrondissement (M° Hôtel de Ville or M° Saint-Paul). Located just north of the Hôtel de Ville and east of the Centre Pompidou, the Marais (especially the **rue des Archives**) is home to much of the gay life in Paris. In most of the establishments here you'll find free weekly and monthly magazines that list everything from the best parties of the week to the best bathhouses to visit. Chances are you'll find something that interests you!

# L'aventure amoureuse

**Christelle est sortie du placard !**
Christelle came out of the closet!

**Christelle est gouine ?!**
Christelle is a lesbian?!

**Qui te l'a dit ?**
Who told you?

**Quoi ?**
What?

**C'est ta sœur Sophie qui me l'a dit.**
Your sister Sophie told me.

**CHRISTELLE ! SOPHIE !**
CHRISTELLE ! SOPHIE !

**ouaf ouaf**
bark bark

## Word Bytes

**l'aventure amoureuse**   the affair *literally, the love adventure*

**sortir du placard/
faire son coming-out**   come out of the closet

### Know-it-all/Tout savoir

*Notice how the dog speaks French! In French, dogs say* **ouaf** *(it sounds like the "waf" in waffle), not "bark" or "woof". Cats, on the other hand, say* **miaou***, which sounds exactly like the English "meow".*

# Use It or Lose It!

Do you know what to say in these situations? Select from the phrases below.

1. You just found out... Jan plays for the other team!
2. You want to know how someone found out Jan plays for the other team.
3. You want to talk in dog language.
4. You want to tell people Jan is out, finally.

**Jan a enfin fait son coming-out**
**Quoi ? Jan est sortie du placard ?!**
**Miaou.**
**Ouaf.**
**Qui te l'a dit ?**

1. Quoi? Jan est sortie du placard ?!
2. Qui te l'a dit ?
3. Ouaf.
4. Jan a enfin fait son coming-out.

# Mixed Up

Put your new vocab to use. Use the LGBT terms to finish the text.

Name a:

a. term for lesbian      b. term for bisexual      c. term for gay

Jérôme and Amélie broke up because Amélie is a _____. She
                                                                a
wanted to date Catherine, the hot blond in her chemistry class. But alas,

Catherine is really *hétéro*, not a _____ nor a _____. After
                                            b                        a
his failure with Amélie, Jérôme thought he might try being _____,
                                                                      c
but after his first date with Jacques he realized that was never going to work.

Poor Jérôme!

# All That Slang

If you're gay, some of these phrases may help you get lucky. If not, read on to be in-the-know on gay culture.

**Mon meilleur ami ♂/Ma meilleure amie ♀ est homosexuel ♂/homosexuelle ♀.**
My best friend is gay.

**Il est actif.**
He's a top.

**Il est passif.**
He's a bottom.

**Je suis versatile.**
I'm versatile. *The French also say **autoreverse** for versatile—just like a tape player.*

**Elle, c'est une camionneuse.**
She's butch.

**J'aime les mecs imberbes.**
I like smooth guys.

**J'aime les ours.**
I like bears. ***Ours** are larger gay men who are hairy and usually have a beard.*

**Les hommes, c'est comme les ours : plus ils sont poilus, mieux c'est.**
Men are like bears: the hairier the better. *This phrase is not specifically gay, but boy is it appropriate for **ours**!*

**C'est une folle.**
He's a queen. *Literally, he's a crazy woman.*

**Il est ambigu ♂/Elle est ambiguë ♀.**
He/She is ambiguous.

**Il marche à voile et à vapeur.**
He plays for both teams.

**C'est où, le bar gay le plus proche ?**
Where's the nearest gay bar?

**Où est la boîte gay ?**
Where's the gay club?

**Allons dans un bar gay.**
Let's go to a gay bar.

**Où est-ce que je peux trouver des drag-queens ?**
Where can I find some drag queens?

**C'est une nana à pédés.**
She's a fag-hag.

**J'adore la Gay Pride à Paris.**
I love the Gay Pride parade in Paris.

**Je suis fier d'être gay !**
I'm proud of being gay!

## Know-it-all/Tout savoir

*Did you notice in some of the phrases above, the female form was used to describe a man? French is a gender-specific language and, in the case of sexuality, speakers can change the gender forms to indicate femininity or masculinity.*

**1.** You've just arrived at a trendy French locale, visit the tourist office, and:
   **a.** ask the clerk: Where is the closest *bar gay*?
   **b.** ask a girl what she's up to *ce soir* while checking out a hot guy.
   **c.** *flirt* with the hot clerk of the opposite sex.

**2.** In the historic part of the city, you notice that the trendiest café has a rainbow flag sticker on the door. You:
   **a.** go in; you know you'll make friends with the cute waiters.
   **b.** walk in, and then sit down—there are a lot of *nanas à pédés* there.
   **c.** go to the sports bar next door to have a beer.

**3.** You arrive at the town's hottest shopping mall and:
   **a.** buy a rainbow flag necklace with a matching nipple ring.
   **b.** you're torn between buying a tight, sexy shirt and a classic buttondown. You end up getting both.
   **c.** invest in a classic outfit—much like the one you're wearing.

**4.** You finally meet that perfect someone for a fling. You've chosen:
   **a.** *une folle* if you're a guy (you like your men like your drinks; delicious and girly) or *une camionneuse* if you're a girl (you prefer your women big and burly).
   **b.** that hot guy from across the room… or is it a hot girl? Who cares!
   **c.** a member of the opposite sex, of course.

**Mostly As:** homosexual
   *Tu es très fier♂/ fiere♀ d'être homo.* Enjoy the gay life, baby!

**Mostly Bs:** bisexual
   You *marche à voile et à vapeur. Ça t'est égal.* You like girls and boys.

**Mostly Cs:** heterosexual
   You're either *hétéro*, straight, or deep in the *placard*.

 **Q&A**

Chère Vivi:
   I've been in Paris for three days now and I feel like everywhere I look the guys are gay. Are there no cute, single, straight guys for me in Paris? Am I in the Twilight Zone?!
                                    Frustrée

Chère Frustrée:
   I know how you feel, but don't get discouraged. Many of the men in France may look gay according to the untrained gaydar, but they're really just metrosexual. They dress in designer clothes, use product in their hair, wear cologne and have a certain *je ne sais quoi* about them. Don't worry, though; many of them are single straight men, so you still have a chance of finding love in Paris!
                 Bonne chance ! (Good luck!),
                                    Vivi

# Use It or Lose It!

Did you pay attention? Do you really know what each phrase means? See if you can pair the phrase with its English equivalent.

1. **Je suis fier d'être gay !**
2. **Mon meilleur ami est gay.**
3. **Elle, c'est une camionneuse.**
4. **J'aime les ours.**
5. **Il marche à voile et à vapeur.**

a. She's butch.
b. My best friend is gay.
c. I'm proud of being gay.
d. He plays on both teams.
e. I like bears.

1. c; 2. b; 3. a; 4. e; 5. d

## Know-it-all/Tout savoir

Gay entertainment is quite popular in the French-speaking world. From gay music stars in the 80's like Dalida and Michou to modern music icons, there's plenty to listen to. Likewise, France also has a long history of great LGBT movies. Even everybody's favorite French actor, Gérard Depardieu, was one of the main characters in the hit gay film, **Le Placard** (The Closet). Below are just a few of the many other gay-themed flicks that you should check out:

# A-List

Top-rated *films gays*, gay-themed flicks...

| | |
|---|---|
| **La Cage aux Folles** | The Birdcage |
| **Ma vie en rose** | My Life in Pink |
| **Comme un garçon** | About a Boy |
| **Gazon maudit** | French Twist |
| **Pédale douce** | *This film has the same title in English; it's a play on words, meaning either a soft pedal (like on a piano) or a gentle fag.* |
| **L'homme blessé** | The Wounded Man |
| **Tenue de soirée** | Evening Dress |

# Love & Dating

## chapter 4

## Get info on:

- how to land a date
- love advice
- anatomy 101
- how to break up with someone
- your love horoscope

##  Dialogue: Julie and Laurent make a *rendez-vous*

Laurent invites Julie out to dinner for their first *rendez-vous*, date…

| | | |
|---|---|---|
| **LAURENT:** | **Salut, Julie, c'est Laurent.** | Hi Julie, it's Laurent. |
| **JULIE:** | **Salut, Laurent, ça va?** | Hey Laurent, how's it going? |
| **LAURENT:** | **Ça va bien. Écoute, qu'est-ce que tu fais vendredi?** | Doing well. Listen, what are you up to on Friday? |
| **JULIE:** | **Pas grand-chose. Pourquoi?** | Not much. Why? |
| **LAURENT:** | **Tu veux dîner avec moi?** | Do you want to have dinner with me? |
| **JULIE:** | **Ouais, ça serait sympa.** | Yeah, that would be nice. |
| **LAURENT:** | **Génial! Je viens te chercher à sept heures.** | Great! I'll come pick you up at 7. |
| **JULIE:** | **Parfait, j'ai trop hâte de te voir!** | Perfect, I can't wait to see you! |

## Word Bytes

| | |
|---|---|
| **aller chercher** | to pick up |
| **faire** | to do |
| **j'ai hâte** | I can't wait |
| **pas grand-chose** | not much |
| **le rendez-vous** | date |
| **vouloir** | to want |

# All That Slang

Things you say when making a date…

| | |
|---|---|
| **Quand est-ce qu'on peut se voir?** | When can we see each other? |
| **J'ai trop hâte de te voir!** | I can't wait to see you! *You might sound a bit desperate, so mind your tone.* |
| **J'attendrai ton coup de fil.** | I'll wait for your call. *Hey! One can wish…* |
| **Je t'appellerai.** | I'll call you. |
| **Ça me ferait trop plaisir!** | I would love to! |
| **On se voit demain.** | We'll see each other tomorrow. |
| **On se voit bientôt.** | We'll see each other soon. |
| **Qu'est-ce que tu fais samedi?** | What are you up to on Saturday? |
| **Tu veux sortir?** | Do you want to go out? *Be straight to the point.* |
| **Arrête de tourner autour du pot, tu m'invites ou quoi?** | Stop beating around the bush—are you going to ask me out or what? |
| **Tu veux passer une nuit de passion avec moi?** | Do you want to have a night of passion? |
| **Bien sûr!** | Of course! |
| **Je viendrai te chercher à neuf heures.** | I'll pick you up at 9. |
| **D'accord, je serai prêt♂/prête♀.** | OK, I'll be ready. |
| **Je peux pas…** | I can't… |
| **Je suis occupé♂/occupée♀.** | I'm busy. |
| **Je dois me laver les cheveux.** | I have to wash my hair. *Nice excuse.* |
| **Et dimanche?** | So what about Sunday? |
| **Tu me tripotes un peu trop là.** | You're touching me too much. |
| **Tu t'approches un peu trop de moi.** | You're getting a little too close to me. |
| **Sans déconner, si tu me touches encore, je te casse la gueule.** | Seriously, if you touch me again I'm going to kick your ass. |

# Use It or Lose It!

Laurent and Julie arranged another *rendez-vous*—but you must arrange their conversation.

| | |
|---|---|
| _____ | **Ça me ferait trop plaisir.** |
| _____ | **Génial, ça marche.** |
| _____ | **Qu'est-ce que tu fais jeudi ?** |
| _____ | **Super, je viendrai te chercher à cinq heures.** |
| _____ | **Et vendredi ? Tu veux sortir ?** |
| _____ | **Je sors avec mes potes.** |

Use these pick-up lines to *draguer*, flirt, at your own risk!

*T'es à tomber.*
You look great.
*Literally, you're to fall for.*

*T'es canon.*
You're hot.

*T'es bien foutu♀/ foutue♂.*
You're fine.

*Salut, je t'offre un verre ?*
Hi, can I buy you a drink?

*T'as un beau cul.* 💣✳
Nice ass.

*Alors, on baise ou quoi ?* 💣✳💣✳
So are we gonna fuck or what?

*Tu peux me montrer comment on roule un patin?*
Can you show me what a real French kiss is?

## Quiz — *Prêt pour la drague?*

Are you ready to hit on a hot French guy or girl?

**1.** You have a date in two hours. You:
   **a.** take a bath, spray on some perfume—all in all, you are *bien habillé ♂ / habillée ♀*.
   **b.** take a shower and then grab something out of the closet; you have to be quick since you don't know where your date lives.
   **c.** watch some TV (hey, you took a bath in the morning, that counts), then walk leisurely to the restaurant.

**2.** When talking to your dates, you usually feel:
   **a.** *calme.*
   **b.** *nerveux ♂ /nerveuse ♀.*
   **c.** *indifférent*—you know there is always going to be another date.

**3.** The pick-up line you use most often to *draguer*:
   **a.** *Salut, je t'offre un verre ?*
   **b.** *T'es à tomber.*
   **c.** *Alors, on baise ?*

**4.** When the date is about to end you:
   **a.** ask *On va se revoir ?* then slip him/her a kiss on the cheek.
   **b.** ask *Qu'est-ce que tu fais vendredi ?*
   **c.** *tripotes* him/her a little too much.

**Mainly As:**
Congratulations—you're a real romantic and should fit in well with the French!

**Mainly Bs:**
You might be ready, but you need more practice.

**Mainly Cs:**
Reschedule. Your manners and attitude need a lot of work before you attempt to win over a French guy or girl.

## Q&A

**Chère Vivi:**
What can I do to have a successful *rendez-vous* with a French speaker?
                                        Robert

**Cher Robert:**
*Sois propre, mets un peu de parfum, décontracte-toi, flirte un peu, blague un peu, ne la/le touche pas trop et amuse-toi bien.* In a nutshell that is all you need to do: be clean, put on a little cologne, relax, flirt a little, joke a little, don't touch too much and have a great time.

Bonne chance!
                                        Vivi

# Word Bytes

In order to have a successful love life, an anatomy lesson is essential.

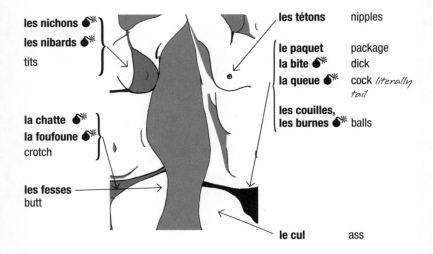

| | |
|---|---|
| **les nichons** 💣✳ | |
| **les nibards** 💣✳ | |
| tits | |
| **la chatte** 💣✳ | |
| **la foufoune** 💣✳ | |
| crotch | |
| **les fesses** | |
| butt | |

| | |
|---|---|
| **les tétons** | nipples |
| **le paquet** | package |
| **la bite** 💣✳ | dick |
| **la queue** 💣✳ | cock *literally tail* |
| **les couilles, les burnes** 💣✳ | balls |
| **le cul** | ass |

# Use It or Lose It!

You've gotta know your body parts. Go ahead and ID 'em.

1. _____

2. _____

3. _____

4. _____

1. les nichons; 2. le cul; 3. le paquet; 4. la chatte

# All That Slang

Terms for foreplay…

| | |
|---|---|
| **embrasser** | to kiss |
| **rouler une pelle/ rouler un patin** | to French kiss *This literally means to roll a shovel or to roll a skate.* |
| **frotter** | to rub |
| **se mettre à poil** | to get naked |

---

All about sex…

| | |
|---|---|
| **faire l'amour** | to make love |
| **coucher ensemble** | to sleep together |
| **baiser, niquer** 💣※ | to fuck |

---

Other sex actions…

| | |
|---|---|
| **sucer** | to suck |
| **tailler une pipe** 💣※ | to give a blowjob |
| **une branlette** | a hand job |
| **jouir** | to finish/to come |

Going solo…

| | |
|---|---|
| **se masturber** | to masturbate |
| **se branler** 💣※ | to jerk off |

---

Positions…

| | |
|---|---|
| **la position du missionnaire** | missionary |
| **en levrette** | doggy style |
| **position Andromaque** | woman on top *Check the Kama Sutra for even more ideas.* |

## Know-it-all/Tout savoir

*Nobody knows who invented French kissing, but the French certainly get credit for it (and boy, are they good at it!). It probably comes from the early 1900s, when the French were thought to be…well…a bit sluttier than the rest of the world. Boy have things changed!*

## Gesture

Are you sleeping with your best friend's girlfriend and he's totally clueless about it? Make this gesture behind his back to tell everyone else that he's *cocu*, being cheated on.

# Use It or Lose It!

Try this fun game of foreplay—in French—with your significant other(s). You'll need dice and the guide below. Each player rolls the dice, says the action aloud in French, then acts it out. Repeat at your leisure. Have fun!

1. **touche ton ♂ / ta ♀ partenaire** — touch your partner
2. **perds un tour** — lose a turn
3. **touche-toi** — touch yourself
4. **embrasse ton partenaire partout** — kiss your partner all over
5. **mets-toi à poil** — get naked
6. **lèche quelque chose** — lick something

# ◀) Une sérénade

## Word Bytes

| | |
|---|---|
| **aimer** | to love |
| **avoir besoin de** | to need |
| **avoir envie de** | to want |
| **se casser** | get the hell out of here (said in anger) |
| **haïr** | to hate |

 **Know-it-all/Tout savoir**

Being **cucul**, means being too cliché, that is, overly romantic and corny to a fault. While the French are definitely romantic, don't go overboard in your attempts at seduction. For example a **sérénade** (serenade) is **cucul**. Sometimes being **cucul** works, sometimes it doesn't. It all depends on you or whom you're dating. Some people like sappy love, some don't.

# Use It or Lose It!

Audrey needs your help to deliver these lines in the correct order. What should she say first, next and last to get rid of Antoine? She also forgot some words, so you'll have to fill in some blanks.

| _____-toi ! | Il est \_\_\_\_\_, ce mec. | Je te \_\_\_\_\_, Antoine. |

# ◀) All That Slang

Talking about *amour* (or getting out of it) is sometimes difficult, especially if you don't know the language. Here are some good-to-know phrases.

| | |
|---|---|
| **Je t'aime.** | I love you. |
| **Je t'aime bien.** | I like you. |
| | *Be careful because it sounds a lot like I love you, but it means much less!* |
| **J'ai envie de toi.** | I want you. |
| **J'ai besoin de toi.** | I need you. |
| **Tu n'as pas envie de moi ?** | You don't want me? |
| **Je te hais./Je te déteste.** | I hate you. |
| **Va-t'en !** | Leave! |
| **C'est pas toi, c'est moi.** | It's not you, it's me. |
| **Connard ♂/Connasse ♀ ! 💣*** | Asshole!/Bitch! |
| **En tout cas, t'es nul au pieu!** | Whatever, you're bad in bed! |

What kind of a relationship are you in—or do you want?!

| | |
|---|---|
| **Je cherche un plan cul.** | I'm looking for a hookup. |
| **On est des potes de baise. 💣*** | We're fuck buddies. |
| **On sort ensemble.** | We're dating. |
| **On est ensemble.** | We're together. |
| **C'est mon copain ♂/ C'est ma copine ♀.** | He's my boyfriend./She's my girlfriend. |
| **On couche ensemble.** | We're sleeping together. |

# Use It or Lose It!

Can you guess the status of these relationships? Write 'em down—in French.

1. Patrick and Sylvie are dating frequently.

2. Michel is just looking to get laid.

3. Matthieu and Aurélie *baisent* occasionally.

4. Arnaud and Caroline only *font l'amour*.

Ils sortent ensemble; 2. Il cherche un plan cul; 3. Ils sont des potes de baise; 4. Ils sont amants.

## Quiz

**Are you a French lover or a heartbreaker? Find out.**

**1.** If your date says he likes you because you have a lot of junk in your trunk, you shout _____ before storming out.
   **a.** *Connard !*
   **b.** *Je t'aime.*
   **c.** *Je te déteste.*
   **d.** A and C

**2.** If you want to tell your partner you really love him/her, say:
   **a.** *Je t'aime.*
   **b.** *J'ai envie de toi.*
   **c.** *Casse-toi !*
   **d.** A and B

**3.** If you want to break up with someone, exclaim:
   **a.** *Va-t'en !*
   **b.** *On couche ensemble.*
   **c.** *Je t'aime bien.*
   **d.** *J'ai envie de toi.*

**4.** If you're looking for a *plan cul*, you want:
   **a.** a one-night stand.
   **b.** a serious relationship.
   **c.** a romantic date.
   **d.** B and C

**5.** You are *cucul* if you:
   **a.** give your partner an awesome gift on their birthday.
   **b.** design a postcard using glitter and send it to your date with a singing telegram.
   **c.** take your date to a fancy restaurant.
   **d.** open the door for your date.

1. d; 2. d; 3. a; 4. a; 5. b

# Ton horoscope

Will you be lucky in love? See what the stars say. In case you get lost:

- Keywords are in bold.
- *Ton chiffre porte-bonheur* = Your lucky number.
- There is a visual guide to colors that complement you.

## Bélier

♈

Tu t'amuseras pendant ton **voyage** et tu rencontreras quelqu'un de très intéressant. Attention ! Ne lui fais pas de compliment sur son **cul** pendant les deux premières minutes !

You'll have a great time on your **trip** and you will meet someone very interesting. Be careful! Don't give any compliments on his/her **ass** in the first two minutes!

Couleur : gris (gray)

Ton chiffre porte-bonheur : sept (7)

## Taureau

♉

Tu vas rencontrer la personne de tes **rêves**, mais elle est déjà **casée**.

You'll meet the person of your **dreams** but he/she is already **taken**.

Couleur : violet (purple)

Ton chiffre porte-bonheur : trois (3)

## Gémeaux

♊

Tu rencontreras des **jumeaux** mais je ne vois pas de plan à trois dans ton avenir. Il faut choisir celui avec qui tu veux **sortir**.

You'll meet **twins**, but I don't see a **threesome** in your future. You have to choose the one that you want **to go out with**.

Couleur : rose (pink)

Ton chiffre porte-bonheur : deux (2)

## Cancer

♋

Tu vas beaucoup **baiser** ⬤*. N'oublie pas d'utiliser des **capotes** !

You're going to **fuck** a lot. Don't forget to use **condoms**!

Couleur : bleu (blue)

Ton chiffre porte-bonheur : un (1)

## Lion

♌

Tu vas découvrir beaucoup de **plaisir** sexuel — mais attention à ne pas devenir **accro** !

You're going to discover a lot of sexual **pleasure**—but be careful that you don't become **addicted**!

Couleur : jaune (yellow)

Ton chiffre porte-bonheur : dix (10)

## Vierge

♍

Si tu es toujours **vierge**, cette semaine ton/ta partenaire **te dépucellera**.

If you're still a **virgin**, this week your partner will **take your virginity**.

Couleur : vert (green)

Ton chiffre porte-bonheur : cinq (5)

## Balance

♎

Essaie de nouveaux **trucs** au **lit**.

Try new **things** in **bed**.

Couleur : blanc (white)

Ton chiffre porte-bonheur : douze (12)

## Scorpion

♏

Quelqu'un va te **pincer** le **cul**. Amuse-toi bien.

Someone will **pinch** your **ass**. Enjoy.

Couleur : orange (orange)

Ton chiffre porte-bonheur : neuf (9)

## Sagittaire

♐

Tu n'as pas de chance en **amour** — peut-être qu'il faut réviser le vocabulaire du chapitre « Going Solo » à la page 39…

You're not lucky in **love**—maybe you should look over the vocab in the "Going Solo" section on page 39…

Couleur : noir (black)

Ton chiffre porte-bonheur : zéro (0)

## Capricorne

♑

Ton♂/Ta♀ partenaire va te **tromper**. Mais ce n'est pas grave puisque tu le/la **trompes** déjà.

Your partner will **cheat** on you. But that's OK because you're **cheating** on him/her already.

Couleur : turquoise (turquoise)

Ton chiffre porte-bonheur : quatre (4)

## Verseau

♒

Il n'est pas conseillé de **faire l'amour** sous l'eau.

It's not recommended that you **make love** under water.

Couleur : marron (brown)

Ton chiffre porte-bonheur : huit (8)

## Poissons

♓

Tu rencontreras ton♂/ta♀ 39ème partenaire ce week-end — enfin le bon !

You'll meet your 39th boyfriend/girlfriend this weekend—finally the right one!

Couleur : argent (silver)

Ton chiffre porte-bonheur : quinze (15)

# Use It or Lose It!

What is your best astrological match?

1. Things are getting kind of boring in bed. Who should you go out with to fix that?

   a. **Balance**
   b. **Taureau**

2. You can't seem to remain faithful in your relationships. Who would be a good match for you?

   a. **Sagittaire**
   b. **Capricorne**

3. If you're looking for someone who has a lot of experience dating, who would be your best match?

   a. **Poissons**
   b. **Gémeaux**

4. Who should be together?

   a. **Cancer et Lion**
   b. **Scorpion et Bélier**

1. a; 2. b; 3. a; 4. a

# Use It or Lose It!

What are their signs—in French?

1. Laure lacks any experience.

2. André has dated a lot of women—and I mean a LOT.

3. Catherine's best color is blue.

1. Vierge; 2. Poissons; 3. Cancer

# Internet

## Get info on:

- working the internet in French
- chatting, instant messaging and blogging
- social networking sites, like Facebook and MySpace

## A high-tech love story

**1** Salut Catherine, ça va ? J'ai trouvé un site Web génial. Je t'ai fait suivre le lien et le mot de passe.

**2** Cool ! Je suis connectée et je regarde mes mails.

**3** Sujet: Vendredi soir ?
De: mec_cool21@HTBXAMOUR.com
A: technofille20@HTBXamour.com
Salut, j'ai vu ton message et j'ai regardé ton profil sur HTBXAMOUR. J'aimerais beaucoup te rencontrer. Est-ce qu'on peut dîner ensemble vendredi soir ? Envoie-moi un mail ou sinon, on peut chatter en ligne.

**4** Il m'a répondu ! Je vais chatter avec lui tout de suite !

**5** Catherine, j'ai un rendez-vous !

**6** Moi aussi !

**7** C'est à sept heures ce soir. Au Café de l'Horloge.

**8** Quoi ?! Tu es mec_cool21@HTBXamour.com ?

**1** Hey Catherine, what's up? I found an awesome website. I forwarded you the link and the password. **2** Cool! I'm online and I'm checking my email. **3** Subject: Friday night? From: mec_cool21@HTBXamour.com To: technofille20@HTBXamour.com Hi, I saw your message and looked at your profile on HTBXAMOUR. I'd love to meet you. Can we have dinner on Friday night? Send me an email, or let's chat online. **4** He wrote me back! I'm going to chat right now! **5** Catherine, I've got a date! **6** Me too! **7** It's at 7 tonight. At the Café de l'Horloge. **8** What!? You're mec_cool21@HTBXamour.com?

47

# Word Bytes

| | | | |
|---|---|---|---|
| **l'adresse** | address | **imprimer** | to print |
| **chatter** | to chat | **le lien** | link |
| **cliquer** | to click | **répondre** | to reply |
| **de** | from | **le site Web** | website |
| **le mail** | e-mail | **supprimer** | to delete |
| **envoyer** | to send | | |
| **être connecté/ être en ligne** | to be online | | |

# Use It or Lose It!

Match the pics with their labels.

cliquer    mot de passe    Je suis connecté.
Je regarde mes mails.

1. _____

2. _____

3. _____

4. _____

a. Je suis connecté; b. Je regarde mes mails; c. cliquer; d. mot de passe

### Know-it-all/Tout savoir

*Did you know that there is no one way to say website in French? Here are the many variations you may see:*

*site*          *page*          *site Web*
*site internet*  *page Web*

# All That Slang

More internet-savvy lingo…

| | |
|---|---|
| **Quel est le lien ?** | What's the link? |
| **Voulez-vous quitter ?** | Are you sure you want to quit? |
| **Voulez-vous vous déconnecter ?** | Do you want to log out? |
| **Elle envoie des SMS jusqu'à ce qu'elle ait mal aux doigts.** | She texts until her fingers hurt. |
| **J'ai chopé un virus et maintenant mon ordi ne marche plus !** | I got a virus and now my computer won't work! |
| **Marc pirate toujours des MP3.** | Marc is always illegally downloading MP3s. |
| **Rechercher sur Google™.** | Search Google™. |
| **J'adore surfer sur le net.** | I love surfing the net. |
| **Mon fournisseur d'accès internet est nul.** | My internet service provider sucks. |
| **Les cookies doivent être activés.** | Cookies must be enabled. |
| **Il faut télécharger un logiciel.** | You have to download a program. |
| **Je n'ai pas de réseau.** | I can't get a (wireless) signal. |
| **Tu peux acheter ça en ligne.** | You can buy that online. |
| **Est-ce que ce café a l'accès WiFi ?** | Does this café have WiFi? |
| **On chattera ce soir.** | We'll chat tonight. |
| **Quel est ton mot de passe ?** | What is your password? |
| **Cliquer sur le bouton.** | Click on that button. |

# Use It or Lose It!

Alice is confused. She wants to talk with Marc about an e-mail she received but she doesn't know the right words. Help her choose the correct words.

| imprimer | site Web | courriel |
|---|---|---|
| lien | envoyé | effacé |

Je voudrais _____ un _____ que Julie m'a
        (print)                          (e-mail)

_____. Le mail contient un _____ d'un
        (sent)                                      (link)

_____ sympa mais je crois que je l'ai _____…
        (website)                                              (erased)

# Can you handle the internet in French?

**1.** If you want to *regarder tes mails*, you type in your:
   **a.** *mot de passe*
   **b.** *lien*
   **c.** *compte*

**2.** If you surf the net frequently (as much as you blink), then someone might call you:
   **a.** *astronaute*
   **b.** *internaute*
   **c.** *geek*

**3.** If the computer suddenly crashes, you scream *merde* and wish you had:
   **a.** *fermé les documents*
   **b.** *téléchargé les documents*
   **c.** *sauvegardé les documents*

**4.** What does it mean to *rechercher* on the net?
   **a.** to search
   **b.** to upload
   **c.** to pirate MP3s

1. a; 2. b although some might call you c; 3. c; 4. a

# Dialogue: Sandrine and Eric

Listen in on Sandrine and Eric, who are having an everyday conversation.

| | |
|---|---|
| SANDRINE: **Allô ?** | Hello? |
| ERIC: **Salut, Sandrine, c'est Eric. Ça va ?** | Hey, Sandrine, it's Eric. How's it going? |
| SANDRINE: **Mon amour, je viens de t'envoyer** | My love, I just sent you an e-mail |

| | | |
|---|---|---|
| ERIC: | **Pas encore une blague pourrie, j'espère...** | Not another dumb joke, I hope... |
| SANDRINE: | **Non, c'est un lien vers Skype™ pour qu'on puisse chatter.** | No, no, it's a link to Skype™, so we can chat. |
| ERIC: | **D'accord, mais je préfère parler au téléphone.** | OK, but I prefer talking on the phone. |
| SANDRINE: | **Qu'est-ce que t'es vieux jeu, toi... Va regarder tes mails.** | You're so old-fashioned... Go check your email. |
| ERIC: | **Ça y est !** | Done! |
| SANDRINE: | **Bon, télécharge le logiciel, comme ça, on pourra chatter.** | Good, go download the program so we can chat. |
| ERIC: | **Okay, à plus.** | OK, talk to you later. |
| SANDRINE: | **Ciao !** | Bye! |

# Dialogue: Sandrine and Eric Text

After downloading the *logiciel*, Sandrine and Eric begin to text.

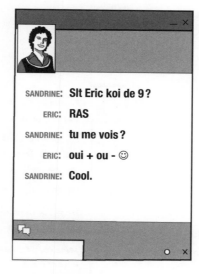

| | |
|---|---|
| SANDRINE: | **Slt Eric koi de 9 ?** |
| ERIC: | **RAS** |
| SANDRINE: | **tu me vois ?** |
| ERIC: | **oui + ou - ☺** |
| SANDRINE: | **Cool.** |

Hey, Eric, what's new?

Nothing.

Can you see me?

Yeah, more or less. ☺

Cool.

# All That Slang

If you want to *chatter* or understand the *SMS/textos*, follow this guide.

| | |
|---|---|
| **koi de 9 = Quoi de neuf ?** | What's new? |
| **ke = que** | that, what, how |
| **c = c'est** | it's |
| **t = t'es** | you're |
| **g = j'ai** | I have |
| **bi1 = bien** | good/well |
| **@+ = à plus** | see you later |
| **RAS = rien à signaler** | nothing's going on |
| **+ = plus** | more |
| **– = moins** | less |
| **2m1 = demain** | tomorrow |
| **a12c4 = à un de ces quatre** | so long |
| **HT = acheter** | to buy |
| **t oqp ? = T'es occupé ?** | Are you busy? |
| **mdr = mort de rire** | LOL *literally, dead from laughing* |
| **qqch = quelque chose** | something |
| **qq1 = quelqu'un** | someone |

*je t'm = Je t'aime.*
I love you.

*biz = bises*
kisses

*tu me mank = Tu me manques.*
I miss you.

*je t'm bcp = Je t'aime beaucoup.*
I love you very much.

*jta = je t'adore*
I adore you.

*bb t où? = Bébé, t'es où?*
Baby where are you?

*t con = Tu es con.*
You're stupid.

*chuis tro cho = Je suis trop chaud.*
💣*💣*
I'm so horny.

*tg = ta gueule* 💣*
Shut the hell up.

*jcherch 1 plan cu = je cherche un plan cul* 💣*
I'm looking for a hookup.

*t chian = t'es chiant* 💣*
You're a pain in the ass.

# Use It or Lose It!

Learn how to text like a pro. Read these texts and translate them to French.

| cedric95: slt koi de 9 ?<br>lori_18: ras et toi ? | cedric95:<br>t tjs a paris ? qq tu fé 2m1 ?<br>lori_18: rien pq ? | cedric95: on fé qqch ?<br>lori_18: ok biz @+ |
|---|---|---|

cedric95: Salut, quoi de neuf ?
lori_18: Rien à signaler, et toi ?
=cedric95: Hey, what's new?
lori_18: Nothing's going on, and what about you?

cedric95: Tu es toujours à Paris ? Qu'est-ce que tu fais demain ? lori_18: Rien, pourquoi ? =cedric95: Are you still in Paris? What are you up to tomorrow? lori_18: Nothing, why?

cedric95: On fait quelque chose ?
lori_18: OK, bises. A plus !
=cedric95: Do you want to do something? lori_18: Okay, kisses. Talk to you later!

# Social networking, en français

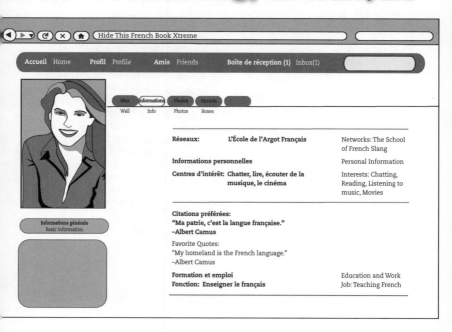

# Use It or Lose It!

Before looking at the Word Bytes section, snoop around our profile...

Can you remember three French words on the Facebook® page that are similar in English?
What does **profil** mean?
What does **accueil** mean?
What are your **centres d'intérêt** and what is your **fonction**?

| | | | |
|---|---|---|---|
| **l'accueil** | start/home | **les groupes** | groups |
| **les amis ajoutés récemment** | recently added friends | **les paramètres** | settings |
| **les applications** | applications | **le profil** | profile |
| **le compte** | account | **la recherche** | search |
| **la déconnexion** | log out | **les réseaux** | networks |

## Q&A

Chère Vivi:
Do people from France use specific social networking sites? I want to meet friends from France and I don't know where to start.

Merci mille fois !
NouveauProfil

Cher NouveauProfil:
*Le réseautage,* or social networking, is definitely cool all over the French-speaking world. Most French speakers use—you guessed it—MySpace® and Facebook®. There are French-specific sites like *On va sortir* (We're going out) or *Trombi,* but they're not nearly as popular.
Some things you can do to give your profile a French flair is to change the language to French and join a language or country-specific MySpace® or Facebook® group. You can also ask your friends to hook you up with French-speaking friends—perhaps you'll find that there truly are just six degrees of separation (or maybe fewer).

Biz,
Vivi

# 🔊 Blogs et Recherches

**1** (Speech bubble) Je vais faire une recherche pour Jean-Paul G., mon « blind date » aujourd'hui.

**2** (Screen)
Blog : Les mecs les plus sexy en France
Thierry Henry, Guillaume Canet, Nicolas Sarkozy, JEAN-PAUL G.
Wikipedia
Article: JEAN-PAUL G., né en 1987…
centerblog.net
Toutes les filles sont amoureuses de JEAN-PAUL G !!!
blogger.com
JEAN-PAUL G. est le meilleur…
unblog.fr
JEAN-PAUL G., le mec le plus canon…

…DING DONG

JEAN-PAUL : Roi des mecs sexy

**3** WAOUH ! Oh… il est là !

**4** Salut, Anne, je suis Jean-Paul.

**1** I'm going to search for Jean-Paul G., my blind date for today. **2** BLOG: The sexiest men in France Thierry Henry, Guillaume Canet, Nicolas Sarkozy, JEAN-PAUL G. Wikipedia Entry: JEAN-PAUL G., born in 1987… centerblog.net All the girls are in love with JEAN-PAUL G. !!! blogger.com JEAN-PAUL G. is the best… unblog.fr JEAN-PAUL G., the hottest guy… **3** WOW! Oh… he's here! **4** Hello, Anne, I'm Jean-Paul.

## Word Bytes

| | | | |
|---|---|---|---|
| **le blog, blogue** | blog | **le blogueur♂/la blogueuse♀** | blogger |
| **bloguer** | to blog | **les recherches♀** | searches |

### Know-it-all/Tout savoir

When typing or texting in French, accented letters may not always display like they're supposed to because some sites or cell phones don't support accented letters. To solve the problem, just leave out the accents. People will understand. Just don't tell your French teacher we told you to leave out the accents or we'll never hear the end of it!

# Use It or Lose It!

Connect the phrases at your highest speed.

1. to blog
2. blogger ♂
3. blog
4. blogger ♀

a. **blogueur**
b. **blogue**
c. **bloguer**
d. **blogueuse**

1. c; 2. a; 3. b; 4. d

# All That Slang

Do you YouTube™? Go ahead—in French.

**Regarde cette vidéo sur YouTube™.**
Check out this YouTube™ video.
*Yep, that's right—French speakers use YouTube™ too!*

**T'as un compte sur YouTube™?**
Do you have a YouTube™ account?

**Vidéos visionnées en ce moment…**
Videos being watched right now…

**Comment est-ce que je peux mettre en ligne une vidéo ?**
How can I upload a video?

**Cette vidéo est trop forte. Je lui ai donné cinq étoiles.**
That video rocks. I gave it a five-star rating.

**Cette vidéo était nulle. Je ne lui donnerais même pas une étoile.**
That video sucked. I wouldn't even give it one star.

**Diffuse cette vidéo.**
Share this video.

**Poster un commentaire.**
Post a text comment.

## Word Bytes

**Rechercher toutes les vidéos**
Search all videos

**Rechercher des vidéos lisibles sur Google™**
Search videos playable on Google™

**Les + (plus) citées dans des blogs**
Most blogged

**Les + (plus) diffusées**
Most shared

**Les + (plus) regardées**
Most viewed

**Les + (plus) fortes progressions**
Movers & Shakers

**Vidéos recommandées**
Recommended videos

**Autres vidéos**
Explore more videos

# Use It or Lose It!

Choose the correct phrase to answer each question.

1. If you want to tell your friend she's gotta see an awesome video you say:
   a. **Regarde cette vidéo sur YouTube™.**
   b. **Les vidéos visionnées en ce moment...**

2. If you want to ask your newest friend if he has a YouTube™ account you say:
   a. **Comment est-ce que je peux mettre en ligne une vidéo?**
   b. **T'as un compte sur YouTube™?**

3. If you thought the video rocked, you say:
   a. **Cette vidéo est trop forte. Je lui ai donné cinq étoiles.**
   b. **Cette vidéo était nulle. Je ne lui donnerais même pas une étoile.**

4. If you thought the video sucked, you say:
   a. **Cette vidéo est trop forte. Je lui ai donné cinq étoiles.**
   b. **Cette vidéo était nulle. Je ne lui donnerais même pas une étoile.**

5. If a video is too cool to keep to yourself, you click on:
   a. **Diffuse cette vidéo.**
   b. **Poster un commentaire.**

1. a; 2. b; 3. a; 4. b; 5. a

## Know-it-all/Tout savoir

Though YouTube™'s default language is English, you can specify your language and country content preferences. Start by clicking on "Worldwide" in the upper right-hand corner and then on "France". Then, click on "English" and change it to **Français**. As you search YouTube™, you'll see French speakers' favorite videos, and what they're watching right now, and the interface will be in French! Also, many of the videos selected will be in French, so you'll have the added bonus of getting immediate access to contemporary French language and visuals.

Google™ Video also has a French interface; go to video.google.fr to immerse yourself in the French world of online videos.

# A-List

Cool and helpful websites for the tech-savvy French speaker…

**www.academie-francaise.fr/dictionnaire**
French dictionary from the *Académie française*

**www.verb2verbe.com**
A French verb conjugator and translator

**www.frenchculture.org**
A website on French culture from the French Embassy

**www.voila.fr**
French search engine

**french.about.com**
Lots of awesome French resources from about.com

**www.zylom.fr**
Games in French

**www.allocine.fr**
A top French movie site

**www.lequipe.fr**
French sports online

**www.pagesjaunes.fr**
The yellow pages of the internet

## Know-it-all/Tout savoir

*Master French technology terms by changing your profile's language and internet settings/preferences to French. Also, when searching online, try fr.yahoo.com (Yahoo!™ France), www.google.fr (Google™ in French). You can also change your computer's default language from English to French. This can usually be done through the Preferences feature. If you wish to go back to English, look for Préférences>Langues>Anglais.*

# Mixed Up

Who hasn't had an embarrassing e-mail mix up like Chloé? Fill in the terms to find out what happens…

a. term for e-mail     c. body part          e. person (relation)
b. place               d. adjective          f. one word text message

Chloé was checking her _____ at the _____. Suddenly,
                              a                                 b

she slipped and a *cliqué* on the wrong button. Her entire contact list received a nasty

message that she meant to send just to her best friend along with a picture of her

_____. After a few minutes, a lot of people had already answered.
        c

Most of them were _____, including her _____, who said
                            d                                      e

_____.
        f

**1.** How many *profils* do you have?
    **a.** I have two, my left and my right.
    **b.** I have two, but I mostly use one.
    **c.** Three that I use and seven that I don't.

**2.** *Un virus* is:
    **a.** a reason to miss a day of school or work.
    **b.** why you avoid opening messages that people *font suivre*.
    **c.** the work of hackers (maybe your own)!

**3.** Your *fournisseur d'accès internet* is:
    **a.** something the phone company charges me for by the minute.
    **b.** DSL.
    **c.** *très haut débit* (broadband).

**4.** *RAM* is:
    **a.** a uncastrated male sheep.
    **b.** something you like to upgrade to keep your computer running smoothly.
    **c.** Random Access Memory or, in French, *mémoire vive*.

**5.** *Les cookies* are:
    **a.** a delicious treat.
    **b.** something your computer stores somewhere for something.
    **c.** maintenance and tracking systems used by HTPS.

**6.** You *regardes* your e-mail:
    **a.** once a week to see if your mom wrote.
    **b.** for work and to send some jokes a few times daily.
    **c.** every five seconds, with your cell phone.

**Mainly As**
You still don't get what all the fuss is about the internet (boy, are you missing out)...

**Mainly Bs**
You are a well-rounded internet user.

**Mainly Cs**
You are an expert. Some may call you *un nerd* but you prefer the term *hacker*.

# Gadgets

# 6

## Get info on:

- names for trendy gadgets
- talking about your cool electronic stuff
- working your cell phone and MP3 player in French

## 🔊 E-junk

**1** I made it! I invented the e-Swiss Army Knife! **2** What? Yeah right... **3** Look, it has a cell phone with a digital camera, Bluetooth™, an MP3 player, WiFi, built-in GPS, e-mail, a keyboard and a touch screen! **4** Philippe, it's exactly like an iPhone® or a Blackberry®, but enormous and awkward. **5** But mine prints... and it uses only 20 AAA batteries.

# 🔊 Word Bytes

**ordinateur**    computer *You can shorten it to just **ordi**.*

---

   **clavier**   keyboard

**ordinateur portable**
laptop
*Not to be confused with
just a **portable**, which is
a cell phone...*

**souris**
mouse

**imprimante**
printer

---

**lecteur CD, DVD et Blu-ray**
CD, DVD and Blu-ray player

**appareil photo
numérique**
digital camera
*You can just say
**appareil photo**.*

**portable** (France)
**cellulaire** (Canada)
**natel** (Switzerland)
cell phone

---

**lecteur MP3**
MP3 player

   **casque, écouteurs**
headphones

**enceinte**
speakers

---

**console de jeux**
Wii™, Playstation®, Xbox™, etc.
*Remember that you can
say these **consoles** in French
with a good French accent!*

**jeux vidéo**
video games

# Use It or Lose It!

Can you find these gadgets in this *mots masqués*?

| | | | |
|---|---|---|---|
| 1. ordinateur | 3. clavier | 5. cellulaire | 7. casque |
| 2. portable | 4. souris | 6. natel | 8. enceinte |

```
T O N V I D E E N C E I N T E C N Y
C O N S O U R I S E O N A T E L R M
P O R T A B L E O M P U T A D A R A
M P U R A T O N M P U M O E N V Y O
L A A U D I F O N C A S Q U E I H K
E N A M O O R D O R D I N A T E U R
O R D E N E R I A L U L L E C R P U
```

## Q&A

Chère Vivi:
   Are there French terms for gadgets like the iPod®?
                                              Merci ! Robert

Cher Robert:
   Many of the gadgets out there retain their English name in French.
There is one difference, though—the pronunciation of the word.

| GADGET | FRENCH PRONUNCIATION |
|---|---|
| GPS | zhay pay ess |
| iPod® | eeh pohd |
| MP3 | ehm pay twrah |
| Palm Pilot® | pahlm |
| PDA | pay day ahh |

Chère Vivi:
   I hear that the keyboards in France are different from the one I use at home. Will I have to learn how to type all over again when I go to *cybercafés*?
                                              Merci beaucoup !
                                              John

Bonjour John:
   It's true—the French use AZERTY keyboards instead of QWERTY. But, most *cybercafés* in France have a QWERTY keyboard available, and you can change the keyboard language on all of their computers. There's a little box in the lower right-hand corner of the screen with "FR" inside it. Click on that and select "EN" to make your AZERTY keyboard type like a QWERTY one.
                                              Bonne chance !
                                              Vivi

# Dialogue: When Gadgets Go Wrong

Hugo calls Hélène to talk about a cool gadget, but the reception is bad...

| | |
|---|---|
| HÉLÈNE: **Allô ?** | Hello? |
| HUGO: **Salut, Hélène, ça va ?** | Hi Hélène, how's it going? |
| HÉLÈNE: **Allô ? Je t'entends mal.** | Hello? I can barely hear you. |
| **Y a pas de réseau ici.** | There's no network here. |
| HUGO: **Tu m'entends ? Ça va ?** | Can you hear me? How's it going? |
| HÉLÈNE: **Alors... tu vas parler ?** | Well... are you going to talk? |
| HUGO: **Oui, Hélène, c'est Hugo.** | Yes, Hélène, it is Hugo. |
| **Je voulais voir si tu avais** | I wanted to see if you bought |
| **acheté le nouveau portable** | the new cell phone with the |
| **avec appareil photo,** | built-in camera, MP3 player and WiFi. |
| **lecteur MP3 et WiFi intégrés.** | |
| HÉLÈNE: **Allô ? T'es là ? J'entends rien.** | Hello? Are you there? I can't hear |
| **Ça coupe.** | anything. It's breaking up. |
| HUGO: **Putain, Hélène. Je te parle.** | Damn it, Hélène, I'm talking to you. |
| **Ce putain de Bluetooth™** | (to himself) This fucking Bluetooth™ |
| **ne marche pas.** | isn't working. |
| HÉLÈNE: **Je t'ai eu ! Je ne suis pas là.** | Got you! I'm not here. |
| **Laissez un message après** | Leave a message after the beep. |
| **le bip sonore.** | |
| RÉPONDEUR: **BIP** | BEEP |
| HUGO: **Hélène, connecte-toi sur** | Hélène, log on to Skype™ ASAP... |
| **Skype™ dès que possible...** | and change this fucking message! |
| **et change ce putain de message !** | |

# Use It or Lose It!

Can you pass the polygraph? Write *vrai* if it's true or *faux* if it's false.

1. Hélène answered the phone, but the connection was bad.
2. "Leave a message after the beep" is *Laissez un message après le bip sonore*.
3. Hugo wants to see if Hélène bought the new and cool cell phone she wanted.

1. faux, Hélène never answered the phone, it was her voicemail message; 2. vrai; 3. vrai.

# Word Bytes

For your cell phone...

**écran** — screen
**menu** — menu
**clavier** — key pad
**touche** — key

| | | | |
|---|---|---|---|
| **appels reçus** | received calls | **mode silencieux** | silent |
| **accède à l'URL** | go to (website) | **mode vibreur** | vibrate |
| **annuler** | cancel | **navigateur** | navigator |
| **appeler** | call | **nouveau message** | new message |
| **appels composés** | dialed calls | **outils** | tools |
| **appels en absence** | missed calls | **paramètres** | settings |
| **bouton de marche** | power button | **profils** | profiles |
| **contacts** | contacts | **raccrocher** | end call |
| **détails** | details | **répondeur** | voice mail |
| **décrocher** | send | **retour** | back |
| **envoyer** | send | **réveil** | alarm |
| **haut-parleur** | speaker phone | **sélectionner** | select |
| **images** | pictures | **silencieux** | mute |
| **jeux** | games | **sonnerie** | ringer |
| **luminosité** | brightness | | |

 **Quiz** — What should you do to...

1. send a text message to your BFF from your *portable?* Click:
   a. *Menu>Messages>Nouveau Message*
   b. *Menu>Message>Boîte de réception*

2. call your friend Amélie? Go to:
   a. *Contacts>Amélie>Appeler*
   b. *Contacts>Amélie>Effacer*

3. turn your phone from ring to vibrate? Click:
   a. *Profils audio>Silencieux*
   b. *Profils audio>Vibreur*

1. a; 2. a; 3. b

**Know-it-all/Tout savoir**

To change your phone to French, go to the settings menu and find "Language" or "International". To get back to English, look for **Paramètres** and then **Langue** to change it back to **Anglais**.

To send a text message go to: **Menu**>**Messages**> **Nouveau Message**>[Type your message]>**Envoyer**.

# Word Bytes

For your MP3 player…

| | |
|---|---|
| **albums** | albums |
| **aléatoire** | shuffle |
| **artistes** | artists |
| **auteurs** | composers |
| **bouton central** | menu button |
| **calendrier** | calendar |
| **chronomètre** | stopwatch |
| **contacts** | contacts |
| **émissions de télévision** | TV shows |
| **films** | movies |
| **genres** | genres |
| **horloge** | clock |
| **jeux** | games |
| **lecture** | play |
| **listes** | playlists |
| **livres audio** | audiobooks |
| **menu** | menu |
| **molette cliquable** | click wheel |
| **morceaux** | songs |
| **musique** | music |
| **notes** | notes |
| **pause** | pause |
| **photos** | pictures, photos |
| **podcasts avec vidéo** | video podcast |
| **podcasts** | podcasts |
| **précédent** | previous |
| **recherche** | search |
| **réglages vidéo** | video settings |
| **réglages** | settings |
| **suivant** | next |
| **vidéo** | video |
| **vidéoclips** | music videos |
| **volume** | volume |

# All That Slang

Gadgets are great, except when they stop working… Here are a few lines you might need when technology works, or when it fails.

| | |
|---|---|
| **Mon ordi n'arrête pas de bugger.** | My computer won't stop messing up. |
| **Faut que j'appelle la hotline.** | I have to call tech support. |
| **L'ordi a un virus.** | The computer has a virus. |
| **Il n'y a plus de pile dans ma souris sans fil.** | There's no battery left in my wireless mouse. |
| **J'ai fait tomber mon portable dans la cuvette des chiottes.** 💣* | I dropped my cell phone in the toilet. *Note that **chiottes** is slang for toilet.* |
| **Il n'y a pas de réseau ici.** | There's no cell phone signal here. |
| **J'ai perdu mon chargeur.** | I lost my charger. |
| **Il faut que je recharge la batterie de mon portable.** | I need to recharge the phone's battery. |
| **Merde, la batterie est morte.** 💣* | Shit, the battery's dead. |
| **Désolé, ça a coupé.** | I'm sorry, I lost the signal. |
| **Je suis tombé directement sur ton répondeur.** | It went straight to your voicemail. |
| **Je dois regarder ma messagerie le plus vite possible.** | I need to check my messages ASAP. |
| **Je conduis. Je passe en mains libres.** | I'm driving. Let me put on my headset. |
| **Son portable est une véritable cabine téléphonique !** | His cell phone is ancient! *Literally, **une véritable cabine téléphonique** is "a true phone booth".* |
| **Tu peux me prêter ton portable ? Il faut que je passe un coup de fil.** | Can I borrow your cell? I need to make a call. |
| **Laisse-moi envoyer ce mail de mon iPhone®.** | Let me send this e-mail from my iPhone®. |
| **Mon iPod® vient de redémarrer tout seul.** | My iPod® just restarted all by itself. |
| **Je dois redémarrer mon iPod®.** | I have to restart my iPod®. |
| **Mon iPod® plante sans arrêt.** | The iPod® is constantly freezing up. |
| **J'ai téléchargé cet MP3 mais il n'est plus dans le dossier.** | I downloaded this MP3 but it's not in the folder anymore. |
| **J'en ai ras le bol de ce putain de portable !** 💣* | I'm tired of this fucking cell! |
| **Putain, j'en ai marre. Il fait chier, cet ordi !** 💣*💣* | I'm so fucking fed up with this. This computer sucks! |

**1.** Your favorite electronic device is:
    **a.** you can't choose—you couldn't live without any of them.
    **b.** you can't decide between your *portable*, your iPod® or your *ordi*.
    **c.** your *micro-ondes*.

**2.** Your *portable* is:
    **a.** a Blackberry® or an iPhone®—you need to be *connecté♂/connectée♀* at all times.
    **b.** a cool one with an *appareil photo* and a *clavier*.
    **c.** standard issue—it came free with the contract.

**3.** You keep your *agenda*:
    **a.** on your Blackberry®, otherwise you couldn't function.
    **b.** on your computer's e-calendar.
    **c.** hanging on your wall...duh. You got it from Mom last year.

**4.** Your *musique* listening schedule is:
    **a.** 24/7. Your iPod® is always *allumé*.
    **b.** occasional. You like to do your chores while listening to your iPod®. Plus, you listen to CDs in the car.
    **c.** infrequent. You have an old *tourne-disque*, record player, at home.

**Mainly As**
You are a child of the digital age. Just make sure you don't forget that there's a whole (real) world outside of your computer room...

**Mainly Bs**
You are a well balanced *mec♂/nana♀*. You use your gadgets to your advantage, but you still need someone to help fix them when they fail.

**Mainly Cs**
Why not take advantage of the digital age and get tech savvy?! Try trading that old Commodore 64® in for a brand new *ordinateur portable*.

## Mixed Up

Write a list of spicy French words you've picked up so far. Then insert them in the text. What happens to Hervé?

a. name of gadget      b. noun      c. infinitive verb      d. plural noun

Hervé broke his _____ and decided to fix it using his _____. Of
                    a                                          b
course it didn't work.  Hervé decided that he would just _____ the thing. That
                                                                      c
didn't work either. "What can I do now?" he thought. "Maybe I'll just throw it in a pile

## chapter 7

# Style

## Get info on:

- French fashion
- decorating your space like a real *Français*

## 🔊 In a Dressing Room

T'as l'air d'une pute dans ce pantalon. On voit ton minou... mais ce décolleté te va trop bien !
You look like a slut in those pants. Your turf is showing... but that low-cut shirt looks great on you!

Tu préfères ce maillot de bain ou ce deux-pièces ?
Do you like this bathing suit or this bikini?

Un maillot une pièce ?! Avec un corps comme le tien, il te faut le deux-pièces !
A one-piece?! With a body like yours, you need the bikini!

CABINES D'ESSAYAGE

Qu'est-ce que tu es beau dans ton smoking... mais il te faut un maillot de corps.
You look handsome in that tux... but you need an undershirt.

Il te faut un autre soutien-gorge et une autre culotte pour cette tenue... on les voit un peu trop, là.
You need different bra and panties with that outfit... they're showing a little too much.

Je ne te permets pas de sortir comme ça !
I'm not letting you go out looking like that!

Mais... mais les chaussettes, le chapeau, et la ceinture vont trop bien ensemble.
But... but, the socks, the hat and the belt go so well together.

# Word Bytes

| | | | |
|---|---|---|---|
| les accessoires | accessories | le maillot de bain | bathing suit |
| la bague | ring | le maillot de corps | undershirt |
| les bottes | boots | le manteau | coat |
| les boucles d'oreille | earrings | la montre | watch |
| le bracelet | bracelet | le pantalon | pants |
| la cabine d'essayage | dressing room | le pull | sweater |
| | | la robe | dress |
| la ceinture | belt | le slip | underpants |
| les chaussettes | socks | le smoking | tux |
| les chaussures | shoes | les sous-vêtements | underwear |
| la chemise | shirt | le soutien-gorge | bra |
| le chemisier | blouse | les talons aiguilles | stilettos |
| le collier | necklace | | |
| le costume/ le tailleur | men's suit/ women's suit | les talons hauts | high heels |
| la culotte | panties | le tee-shirt | T-shirt |
| la jupe | skirt | la tenue | outfit |
| les lunettes de soleil | sunglasses | la veste, le blouson | jacket |

# Use It or Lose It!

In what order do you put on your clothes (assuming you're NOT a superhero)? Put each list of clothes in the right order.

1. **pull, maillot de corps, manteau**
2. **chaussures, pantalon, slip**
3. **culotte, talons aiguilles, jupe**

3. culotte, jupe, talons aiguilles
2. slip, pantalon, chaussures
1. maillot de corps, pull, manteau

# All That Slang

| | |
|---|---|
| Ça a l'air beau/moche. | It looks good/ugly. |
| Ce pantalon est chic. | Those pants are chic. |
| Cette jupe est sexy. | This skirt is sexy. |
| Cette chemise est élégante. | This shirt is elegant. |
| Ces chaussures sont horribles. | These shoes are horrible. |
| Ce jean est trop serré. | These jeans are too tight. |
| Ton décolleté est trop plongeant. | There's too much cleavage. |
| Cette jupe est trop courte ; on voit tes fesses. | That skirt is too short; we can see your ass. |
| Ce chemisier est transparent. | That blouse is see-through. |
| T'es assez dénudé♂/dénudée♀. | You're showing too much skin. |
| Elle/Il a l'air ridicule ! | She/He looks ridiculous! |
| Qu'est-ce que c'est que ce look ? | What's up with that look? |
| Elle s'est regardée dans la glace ? | Did she look in the mirror? |
| Cette chemise ne va pas avec ce pantalon. | That shirt doesn't go with those pants. |
| C'est quoi, cette tenue ? | What the heck are you wearing? |
| Remonte ton pantalon, on voit tes fesses. | Pull up your pants, your ass is showing. |
| Ta braguette est ouverte. | Your fly's open. |

*J'adore ton pull !*
I love your sweater!

*Cette robe est magnifique !*
That dress is beautiful!

*Ce jean te va trop bien !*
Those jeans look so good on you!

*Cette robe est trop moche.*
That dress is so ugly.

*C'est ta maman qui t'a fringué♂/fringuée♀ comme ça ?*
Did your mommy dress you like that?

*T'as l'air d'une pute, habillée comme ça.* ☀
You look like a slut dressed like that.

Do you know what to wear in order to be *bien sapé* ♂ /*bien sapée* ♀ ?

*Tu t'habilles comment pour…?*
What do you wear to…?

**1.** *aller à un entretien d'embauche* (a work interview)
   **a.** *jean, maillot de corps, pull*
   **b.** *chemisier/chemise, pantalon*
   **c.** *un smoking*

**2.** *aller à un gala* (a gala)
   **a.** *jean, tee-shirt*
   **b.** *costume, cravate* (tie)
   **c.** *une robe longue avec des talons hauts Manolo Blahnik*

**3.** *aller en boîte* (a night club)
   **a.** *jogging* (jogging suit)
   **b.** *jupe, talons hauts*
   **c.** *une tenue à la* Sex and the City

**4.** *faire du camping* (go camping)
   **a.** *jupe, talons aiguilles*
   **b.** *jean, sweat-shirt*
   **c.** *manteau de fourrure* (fur coat)

**5.** *aller au centre commercial* (the mall)
   **a.** *maillot de bain, chapeau*
   **b.** *jean, chemisier/chemise*
   **c.** *vêtements de marque*

**Mostly As**
   You have no idea of what is appropriate. Still, you feel comfortable in your clothes and that's what really matters.

**Mostly Bs**
   You dress appropriately, but you're not going to be on the cover of a magazine any time soon.

**Mostly Cs**
   You really know your fashion! But be careful, you might overdo it sometimes, not to mention the hole your dressing habits leave in your pockets.

# Use It or Lose It!

The paparazzi are working a new festival in Cannes: The Xtreme French Music Awards. You're the Fashion Police. What will you say about each artist? Write a phrase from the phrase box in the speech bubbles underneath each artist. For extra points, try to identifying each piece of clothing.

- a. Ce pantalon est trop grand pour toi.
- b. Ces chaussures sont horribles et elles ne vont pas avec cette robe.
- c. Elle a l'air ridicule !
- d. Tu t'es regardé dans la glace ?
- e. Cette jupe est trop courte ; on voit tes fesses.
- f. Ton décolleté est trop plongeant.

And there's only one thing to say about that photographer on the left, whose huge crack is visible:

**On voit ses fesses !**

1.d ; 2.b ; 3.f ; 4.a ; 5.c ; 6.e

73

# ⏺ Top Décorateur

**1** Bonjour, et bienvenue à *J'échange ma maison*. Dans cet épisode, les sœurs Dupont ont échangé leurs maisons et changé la déco des pièces. Voyons ce qu'elles en pensent.

**Le salon et la cuisine de Laura: Avant**
Laura's living room and kitchen: Before

**Le salon et la cuisine de Laura: Après**
Laura's living room and kitchen: After

**2** J'adore ce que tu as fait chez moi. Les appareils électroménagers sont les modèles les plus récents. Tout est magnifique !
Le canapé est confortable. J'aime bien la combinaison des couleurs.

**3** Mon style est éclectique et j'ai été inspiré par la plage.

**La chambre de Camille: Avant**
Camille's Bedroom: Before

**La chambre de Camille: Après**
Camille's Bedroom: After

**4** Il y a un tableau de ta famille et un miroir au plafond.

**5** C'est trop kitsch. Ça ne me plaît pas... Je veux ma maison comme avant.

**6** Le lit est joli...

**1** Hello, and welcome to *Trading Houses*. In this episode, the Dupont sisters traded houses and redecorated each other's rooms. Let's see what they think! **2** I love what you did with the house. The kitchen appliances are the newest models. Everything's incredible! The sofa is comfortable. I love the color combination. **3** My style is eclectic and my inspiration was the beach. **4** It has a painting of your family and a mirror on the ceiling. **5** It's so tacky. I don't like it... I want my house like before. **6** The bed is pretty...

# Use It or Lose It!

Can you pass the polygraph? Write *vrai* if it's true and *faux* if it's false.

1. Laura hates her *salon*.
2. Camille adores her *chambre*.
3. There is a *lit* in Laura's room.
4. The *cuisine* is the place where you cook.

1. faux; 2. faux; 3. faux; 4. vrai.

# Word Bytes

Some items and phrases you might have seen on *Je change de maison*...

| | |
|---|---|
| **les appareils électroménagers** | household appliances |
| **l'art** | art |
| **la bibliothèque** | bookcase |
| **les bougies** | candles |
| **C'est trop kitsch !** | It's so tacky! |
| **le canapé** | sofa |
| **la chaise** | chair |
| **la chambre** | bedroom |
| **la combinaison des couleurs** | color combination |
| **le congélateur** | freezer |
| **la cuisine** | kitchen |
| **la cuisinière** | stove top |
| **décorer** | decorate |
| **l'évier** | sink |
| **la fenêtre** | window |
| **le four** | oven |
| **le frigo** | refrigerator |
| **le goût** | taste |
| **l'inspiration** | inspiration |
| **la lampe** | lamp |
| **le lit** | bed |

| | |
|---|---|
| **le lustre** | chandelier |
| **la maison** | house, home |
| **les meubles** | furniture |
| **le micro-ondes** | microwave |
| **le miroir** | mirror |
| **Mon style est... minimaliste/ éclectique/ moderne/ classique.** | My style is... minimalist/ eclectic/ modern/ classic. |
| **le mur** | wall |
| **l'oreiller** | pillow |
| **la pièce, la salle** | room |
| **le placard** | closet |
| **le plafond** | ceiling |
| **la porte** | door |
| **les rideaux** | curtains |
| **le salon** | living room |
| **la table** | table |
| **la table basse** | coffee table |
| **la table de chevet** | night table |
| **le tableau** | painting |
| **le ventilateur** | fan |

# Use It or Lose It!

What's up with *la chambre de Camille*? ID each hideous item in French.

1. bed
2. curtain
3. pillow
4. window
5. painting
6. fan
7. mirror

1. lit; 2. rideaux; 3. oreiller; 4. fenêtre;
5. tableau; 6. ventilateur; 7. miroir

## Quiz — *Qu'est-ce qui va mieux...?*

What would look better...?

**1.** in the red living room
   **a.** *un canapé bleu* with polka-dots
   **b.** *un canapé* in leather *blanc*

**2.** in the bedroom
   **a.** *un frigo*
   **b.** *une table de chevet*

**3.** on the patio
   **a.** *des rideaux*
   **b.** *une piscine*

**4.** in the kitchen
   **a.** *une table basse*
   **b.** *un plan de travail en granit*

**Mostly As:** *Tu as mauvais goût*
Please hire a designer; doing it yourself could be detrimental to your home.

**Mostly Bs:** *Tu as bon goût*
Are you a *décorateur*, designer, or just naturally savvy with design?

## Word Bytes

| | | | | | | | |
|---|---|---|---|---|---|---|---|
| **blanc** | white | **gris** | gray | **rouge** | red |
| **bleu** | blue | **jaune** | yellow | **vert** | green |
| **brun/ marron** | brown | **noir** | black | **violet** | purple |
| | | **rose** | pink | | |

What do ya think of those colors? Put one of these after a color to describe it.

| | | | |
|---|---|---|---|
| **clair** | light | **pastel** | pastel |
| **fluo** | fluorescent | **vif** | bright |
| **foncé** | dark | | |

# Health

## chapter 8

## Get info on:
- relaxation: mind and body
- gross bodily functions
- STDs and other issues

## All That Slang

Stressed out? Get it off your chest.

| | |
|---|---|
| **Je suis tout tendu♂/toute tendue♀.** | I'm all tense. |
| **Il faut que tu te décontractes un peu.** | You need to relax a little. |
| **Le travail et la fac/l'école me rendent fou♂/folle♀.** | Work and college/school are driving me crazy. |
| | *L'école is a general term for school, while la fac, short for faculté, or l'université means college. Be careful—if you tell a French person you're in college, that means you're in middle school!* |
| **Je pète un plomb.** | I'm losing it. |
| | *Literally, I'm blowing a fuse.* |
| **Respire profondément. Inspire, expire.** | Breathe deeply. Inhale, exhale. |
| **Tu veux faire du yoga ?** | Do you want to do yoga? |
| **Je ne suis pas très souple.** | I'm not very flexible. |
| **Est-ce qu'on devrait aller au club de gym ?** | Should we go to the gym? |
| **Oh là là, t'as l'air stressé♂/stressée♀.** | Wow, you look stressed. |
| **Décontracte-toi. Sois heureux♂/heureuse♀.** | Relax. Be happy. |
| **Mon amour, mets-toi à l'aise, je vais te faire un massage complet.** | My love, get comfortable, I'm going to give you a head-to-toe massage. |
| **Tu devrais te décontracter ; le stress te donne des rides.** | You should relax, stress gives you wrinkles. |

# ◉Use It or Lose It!

*Décontracte-toi !* Just follow this *exercice pour se décontracter* and feel your tensions melt. For XTREME relaxation, see if you can follow the audio instructions without peeking at the book.

| | |
|---|---|
| **Trouve une position confortable.** | Find a comfortable position: |
| **Assieds-toi ou allonge-toi et décontracte-toi.** | Sit down or lie down, and relax. |
| **Inspire un grand coup et expire.** | Take a deep breath in and out. |
| **Inspire,** | Inhale, |
| **retiens ta respiration,** | hold your breath |
| **et expire.** | and exhale. |
| **Continue à respirer à fond.** | Keep breathing deeply. |
| **Maintenant, lève-toi.** | Now stand up. |

# Use It or Lose It!

*Le stress te tue ?* Is stress killing you? These people are hurting too. Join each situation with the phrase that describes it.

1. Marc has too much homework. He says...

2. Pierre cannot reach his toes during yoga. He says...

3. Alice is stressing about everything. Your obligation as a friend is to warn her...

4. What you wish your boyfriend or girlfriend would say to you after a long day...

5. Benoît did not do the relaxation exercises for his *muscles*. Now he is complaining...

6. You notice your friend is too stressed. You suggest...

a. **Je suis tout tendu.**

b. **La fac me rend fou.**

c. **Tu veux faire du yoga ?**

d. **Je ne suis pas souple.**

e. **Tu devrais te décontracter, le stress donne des rides.**

f. **Mon amour, mets-toi à l'aise, je vais te faire un massage complet.**

1. b; 2. d; 3. e; 4. f; 5. a; 6. c.

# All That Slang

Health isn't just about relaxation and stress. Here's the grosser side of taking care of your body.

**Je vais me chier/pisser dessus.** 💣* 💣*

I'm gonna shit/pee myself. *Use this one when you really need a bathroom.*

**J'ai la chiasse. Où sont les toilettes ?** 💣*

I have the runs. Where's the bathroom?

**Merde, il n'y a plus de PQ !**

Shit, there's no more TP! **PQ=papier cul** (ass paper)

**Berk ! Qui a pété ?**

Yuck! Who farted?

**J'ai le visage couvert de boutons.**

My face is full of pimples.

**J'ai des crottes qui sortent du nez.**

I've got snot coming out of my nose. *Another term for snot is* **la morve**.

**Il a balancé un grand crachat.**

He spit a big loogey.

**J'ai un rhume carabiné.**

I have a terrible cold.

**Ce repas m'a fait dégueuler.** 💣*

This meal made me hurl. **Dégueuler** *is a crude way of saying to throw up. If you need to be a little more polite, try* **vomir**.

**J'ai trop bu hier soir, et maintenant, j'ai la gueule de bois.**

I drank too much last night and now I have a hangover.

**J'ai mal au ventre/au dos/à la tête.**

My tummy/back/head hurts.

And for those special, below the belt, health situations:

**T'as une capote ?**

Do you have a condom?

**Cet enfoiré m'a refilé des morpions.** 💣*

That asshole gave me crabs.

**Je déteste les MST.**

I hate STDs. *The term for STD is* **MST**. *It means* **maladie sexuellement transmissible**.

## Know-it-all/Tout savoir

*The French are much more liberal about sexuality than many other cultures. What happens if you're ready to go all the way and forgot to bring a condom? Well, you just go down to the street and find one of the ubiquitous condom dispensers—just make sure you have some change!*

## Know-it-all/Tout savoir

When one of your friends sneezes, be polite and say **À tes souhaits**, which means "to your wishes". If he/she sneezes a second time in a row, you say **À tes amours**, "to your loves" and if he/she is equally polite, the response will be **que les tiennes durent toujours**, which means "may yours last forever".

## Quiz — What would you say when...?

**1.** You're out of TP:
 **a.** Merde, il n'y a plus de PQ!
 **b.** Nothing, you just use a receipt you have in your wallet.
 **c.** Je me chie dessus !

**2.** Someone sneezes:
 **a.** À tes souhaits !
 **b.** Nothing. You don't want to open your mouth and catch their germs.
 **c.** Merde !

**3.** Someone farts:
 **a.** Berk ! Qui a pété ?
 **b.** What is that funky smell?
 **c.** Cet enfoiré m'a refilé des morpions.

**4.** Your head aches, your body is producing excessive amounts of snot and you're coughing and sneezing like crazy:
 **a.** J'ai un rhume carabiné.
 **b.** I feel miserable.
 **c.** J'ai le visage couvert de boutons.

**5.** You make a pit stop at the pharmacy before an X-rated date:
 **a.** T'as une capote ?
 **b.** I hope you have extra large condoms.
 **c.** J'ai la chiasse. Où sont les toilettes ?

**Mostly As**
 Good for you, you really know your slang!

**Mostly Bs**
 You really should try to speak more French; you never know how much you've learned until you try it.

**Mostly Cs**
 You have no idea what's going on in any language. Careful! You might catch something nasty.

# Go Green

## chapter 9

## Get info on:
- being green, French style

## 🔊 Être écolo

**Avez-vous besoin d'un sac en plastique ?**
Do you need a plastic bag?

**Non, merci, j'ai mon propre cabas.**
No thanks, I have my own shopping bag.

**Chéri, le bac à compost pue trop.**
Honey, the compost bin stinks too much.

**Oh oui, ça sent la merde.**
Yeah, it smells like shit.

**Je déteste réutiliser... surtout les fringues de ma sœur.**
I hate reusing... especially my sister's clothes.

**À qui le dis-tu ! Il n'y avait pas de PQ...**
Tell me about it! There was no TP...

**Berk ! En plus, il n'y a pas d'eau chaude...**
Yuck! Plus there is no hot water...

# ◉ All That Slang

*Écologique*, green, lingo that you've gotta know…

| | |
|---|---|
| **Que peut-on faire pour améliorer l'environnement ?** | What can we do to improve the environment? |
| **Peut-on faire du covoiturage dans ta voiture hybride ?** | Can we carpool in your hybrid? |
| **L'environnement est foutu.** 💣* | The environment is fucked. |
| **Il y a beaucoup de pollution.** | There's a lot of smog. |
| **Putain, il fait chaud ! Ça doit être l'effet de serre.** 💣* 💣* | Damn it's hot! It must be the greenhouse effect. |
| **Merde ! J'ai oublié d'apporter mon cabas.** 💣* | Oh crap! I forgot to bring my own shopping bag. |
| **Chantal réutilise toujours la même bouteille d'eau.** | Chantal always reuses the same water bottle. |
| **David prend toujours son café dans un thermos.** | David always gets his coffee in a travel mug. |

# Use It or Lose It!

Do you really know your *écologique* lingo? Join the phrases to prove it.

a. **Que peut-on faire pour améliorer l'environnement ?**

b. **Tu peux me conduire quelque part dans ta voiture hybride ?**

c. **L'environnement est foutu.**

d. **Il y a beaucoup de pollution.**

e. **Putain, il fait chaud ! Ça doit être l'effet de serre.**

f. **Elle réutilise toujours la même bouteille d'eau.**

g. **As-tu un thermos ?**

1. She always reuses the same water bottle.

2. The environment is fucked.

3. Can you give me a ride in your hybrid?

4. What can you do to improve the environment?

5. There is a lot of smog.

6. Damn, it's hot! It must be the greenhouse effect.

7. Do you have a travel mug?

a.4; b.3; c.2; d.5; e.6; f.1; g.7

# Quiz  *Es-tu écolo?*

**1.** At the end of a meal, you:
  **a.** wash the dishes by hand, with *un liquide vaisselle écologique* (eco-friendly soap).
  **b.** put the dishes in the dishwasher, but wait until it's full to turn it on.
  **c.** throw everything in the garbage, plates and all. Hey, that's what paper plates are for, right?

**2.** When you go to *le supermarché* (the supermarket) you:
  **a.** bring your own *sacs*.
  **b.** request *sacs en plastique*, paper bags, and reuse them later.
  **c.** get plastic bags and double bag them in paper bags. It's free, plus you wouldn't want anything to rip or break!

**3.** When you go on vacation, you:
  **a.** always reuse your towels and sheets.
  **b.** make sure to turn off the lights and air conditioning in your hotel room when you leave for the day.
  **c.** live it up—there's no excess you can't handle!

**4.** You get around:
  **a.** by *vélo* (bike) or *à pied* (by foot).
  **b.** *voiture hybride* (hybrid) or *transports en commun* (public transportation).
  **c.** SUV—you love that Hummer.

**5.** When you eat, you:
  **a.** use silverware, ceramic plates and cloth napkins, then you make a *bac à compost* with the leftovers.
  **b.** use your own plates, but you always use paper napkins.
  **c.** use paper plates, and you double them so they don't leak.

**6.** You use your *climatisation*, air conditioning:
  **a.** only if it's more than 100°F. You can handle heat waves with water, quick cold showers and maybe a low-voltage fan while you are sleeping.
  **b.** for sleeping only. You go to the beach or the mall during the day to beat the heat.
  **c.** *tous les jours*, every day! There's a reason why they exist, and you don't mind the electric bill.

**Mostly As:** *Tu es écolo !*
You are as green as a tree in *printemps* (spring). If recycling were a religion, you would be the pope.

**Mostly Bs:** Écolo in the making
You're trying to be green while maintaining some type of comfort. You're helping the environment by doing your part and it's worth it.

**Mostly Cs:** *Assassin d'arbres*
Among other things, you are a "tree assassin". You better change your ways—Mother Nature might just take your wastefulness personally.

# Travel

## chapter 10

## Get info on:

- must-see places
- the cash you need
  in French-speaking countries
- hotel lingo
- bar and club lingo
- tasty treats and trendy drinks
- shopping

## 🔊 Les photos de vacances

Élodie is real forgetful and she's always misplacing things. For example, she just found an SD card from her digital camera with hundreds of pictures from various vacations. Now she's going through the photos and trying to figure out where she was and what she was doing.

**Oh oui, je m'en souviens bien. J'ai fait une croisière avec ma famille, je me suis fait bronzer à la piscine, et j'ai été malade !**
Oh, I remember this well. I went on a cruise with my family, I tanned out by the pool, and I got sick!

Je suis allée à Nice avec ma sœur. Nous avons séjourné dans un petit hôtel de luxe et nous avons passé toute la journée à la plage. C'était vachement sympa !

I went to Nice with my sister. We stayed in a boutique hotel and spent all day on the beach. It was so nice!

Oh, j'ai adoré les musées de Paris quand j'y suis allée avec ma classe. Je n'ai toujours pas vu tout ce qu'il y a à voir au Louvre.

Oh, I loved the museums in Paris when I went there with my class. I still haven't seen everything there is to see in the Louvre.

J'ai fait un voyage à Montréal avec mon copain Loïc. On a fait du tourisme et on s'est paumés dans la ville. Loïc n'aime pas demander son chemin.

I went on a trip to Montreal with my boyfriend Loïc. We went sightseeing and got lost in the town. Loïc doesn't like to ask for directions.

J'ai fait un safari dans la jungle… mais je n'ai pas vu beaucoup d'animaux.

I went on a safari in the jungle… but I didn't see a lot of animals.

J'ai fait une randonnée en Corse. C'était génial. J'adore l'aventure !

I went backpacking in Corsica. It was awesome. I love adventure!

J'ai fait du ski dans les Alpes avec mes amis. Qu'est-ce qu'il faisait froid !

I went skiing in the Alps with my friends. It was so cold!

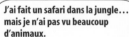

85

# Use It or Lose It!

Élodie has finally posted all of her vacation pics to her blog and now she needs to add a description to each picture. Can you help her?

a.

b.

c.

d.

e.

f.

g.

1. **J'ai fait un safari dans la jungle.**

2. **J'ai fait du tourisme avec mon copain à Montréal.**

3. **J'ai fait une randonnée en Corse.**

4. **J'ai fait une croisière avec ma famille.**

5. **J'ai visité les musées de Paris avec ma classe.**

6. **J'ai fait du ski dans les Alpes.**

7. **J'ai séjourné dans un hôtel de luxe avec ma sœur à Nice.**

1. e; 2. d; 3. f; 4. a; 5. c; 6. g; 7. b

---

Are you a nice tourist or a naughty one?

*aller à la plage*, go to the beach

get a *verre*, drink, in a local *bar*

meet *quelqu'un*, someone, at a club

*voir un film*, see a movie

*parler avec*, talk to a local in his or her language

*aller à une plage de nudistes*, go to a nudist beach

get *bourré♂/bourrée♀*, drunk, in a local *bar*

go back to your hotel room with *quelqu'un* you just met

*voir*, see, a peep show (which is just *peep show* in French too!)

*insulter*, insult a local in his or her language

86

# A-List

Top 15 things to do in France…

1. Visit Paris, also known as the *ville lumière*, or "Light City".
2. Go to the top of the *Tour Eiffel*, the Eiffel Tower.
3. Spend eight days walking around the Louvre—that's how long you need to see everything—and make sure you don't miss *la Joconde*, the Mona Lisa.
4. Sit on the terrace of a café and sip some *vin*, wine, or have a *café*, coffee.
5. Take a stroll through any French city during the *Fête de la Musique*, Festival of Music.
6. Visit Versailles, the gargantuan palace built for Louis XIV.
7. Climb the bell tower of Notre-Dame de Paris and see if you can find the hunchback.
8. Ski or snowboard in the French Alps.
9. Eat something new: *escargots*, snails, or *boudin noir*, blood sausage.
10. Visit one of the many wineries throughout the country.
11. Go sunbathing on the beautiful beaches of the French Riviera.
12. Go surfing in Biarritz, the surfing capital of Europe.
13. Take a scenic trip visiting the *châteaux*, castles, of the Loire River Valley.
14. Go hiking or backpacking in Corsica.
15. Go to Nice to celebrate Mardi Gras in its 10-day *carnaval*.

# Use It or Lose It!

Camille did the Xtreme vacation tour. Name the can't-miss experience in each picture from Camille's vacation album.

1.

2.

3.

4.

5.

1. La Tour Eiffel
2. Le Louvre
3. Les Alpes
4. Les escargots
5. La Fête de la Musique

# ◉Dialogue: Monsieur Trompe arrives at Hotel V

Hotel V is *un petit hôtel de luxe* in the imaginary city of Saint-Croissant. Check out its awesome amenities. M. Trompe, an annoying first-time client, is checking in.

| | | |
|---|---|---|
| **ÉLISE:** | **Bienvenue, Monsieur Trompe. Vous êtes dans la chambre Warhol avec vue sur la mer.** | Welcome Mr. Trompe. Your room is the Warhol, with a sea view. |
| **M. TROMPE:** | **Merci. Dites, Élise, est-ce qu'il y a une connexion Wifi dans la chambre ?** | Thanks. Hey, Élise, is there wireless internet in the room? |
| **ÉLISE:** | **Oui, dans tout l'hôtel. Il y a également des jeux vidéo et des films gratuits.** | Yes, everywhere in the hotel. There are also free video games and movies. |
| **M. TROMPE:** | **Est-ce qu'il y a d'autres équipements ?** | Are there other amenities? |
| **ÉLISE:** | **Il y en a beaucoup ! Il y a un bar, un restaurant à fondue, un spa, une piscine, un centre d'affaires, trois salles de conférence, un service d'étage, un gymnase, un service de baby-sitting, un service de blanchisserie, un service de voiturier, un service de location de portable et de vélo et beaucoup d'autres choses ! Voici un prospectus avec tous ces renseignements.** | There are a lot. There's a bar, a fondue restaurant, a spa, a pool, a business center, three conference rooms, room service, a gym, a babysitting service, dry-cleaning, valet parking cell phone and bike rental and many other things! Here's a brochure with all the info. |
| **M. TROMPE:** | **Et est-ce que je peux prendre le shampooing de l'hôtel ?** | And, may I take the hotel's shampoo? |
| **ÉLISE:** | **Bien sûr.** | Of course. |
| **M. TROMPE:** | **Waouh, quel bel hôtel !** | Wow, what a great hotel! |
| **M. TROMPE:** | **Une dernière chose, où se trouve l'ascenseur ?** | One last thing, where's the elevator? |

| | | |
|---|---|---|
| ÉLISE: | **Ah non, il n'y a pas d'ascenseur…** | Oh no, there isn't one… you have to |
| | **il faut prendre l'escalier.** | take the stairs. |
| M. TROMPE: | (to himself) **Fait chier! Il n'y a** | What the fuck?! There's no fucking |
| | **pas de putain d'ascenseur** | elevator in this shitty hotel?! |
| | **dans cet hôtel de merde !?** 💣✳💣✳ | |

# Word Bytes

| | |
|---|---|
| **beaucoup** | a lot |
| **le centre d'affaires** | business center |
| **la chambre** | room |
| **les choses** | things |
| **la connexion Wifi** | wireless internet connection |
| **dans tout l'hôtel** | everywhere in the hotel |
| **les équipements** | amenities |
| **les films** | movies |
| **gratuit♂/gratuite♀** | free |
| **l'hôtel** | hotel |
| **il y a** | there is, there are |
| **les jeux vidéo** | video games |
| **la location** | rental |
| **le mec** | guy, dude |
| **la mer** | sea |
| **la piscine** | pool |
| **le portable** | cell phone |
| **poser une question** | to ask a question |
| **le prospectus/la brochure** | brochure |
| **la salle de conférence** | conference room |
| **le séjour** | stay |
| **le service d'étage** | room service |
| **le service de blanchisserie** | dry cleaning |
| **le service de voiturier** | valet parking |
| **le vélo** | bike |
| **la vue** | view |

# Use It or Lose It!

The Hotel V quality department is keeping tabs on Élise to asses her service. Help them fill in the blanks in this phone call made from a *portable* with poor reception.

ÉLISE: Hôtel V, bonsoir.

FRANK: Bonsoir, est-ce qu'il y a une connexion Wifi dans la _____ (room)?

ÉLISE: Oui, _____ (everywhere in the hotel). _____ (There are) aussi des jeux vidéo et des films _____ (free).

FRANK: Est-ce qu'il y a d'autres _____ (amenities)?

ÉLISE: Il y a un bar, un spa, une _____ (pool), un _____ (business center), un _____ (valet parking), un _____ (room service), un _____ (rental) de portable et de vélo et beaucoup d'autres _____ (things).

FRANK: Quel bel _____ (hotel)!

chambre; dans tout l'hôtel; Il y a; gratuits; équipements; piscine; centre d'affaires; service de voiturier; service d'étage; service de location; choses; hôtel;

# All That Slang

We don't recommend you travel with every single item listed below, but here's how to say the different pieces of luggage in French:

| | |
|---|---|
| **bagages** | luggage |
| **valise** | suitcase |
| **sac à dos** | backpack |
| **sac à main** | purse |
| **bagage à main** | hand baggage/carry-on bags |
| **sac marin** | duffel bag |

Chère Vivi:
  Instead of staying in a typical, hotel, I want to try something different on my trip to France. What do you suggest?
                              Merci,
            Aventureux (Adventurous)

Cher Aventureux:
  Apart from hostels, *les* *auberges de jeunesse*, you can try renting an apartment. They're usually cheaper than hotels, you have more privacy and most of them have kitchens so you can save money by making your own food.
            Amuse-toi bien! (Have fun!)
                              Vivi

When you travel, you:

**1. a.** speak English to everyone—somebody is bound to understand you.
  **b.** learn some phrases in the country's language—especially the naughty ones!
  **c.** learn the language and memorize your Hide This Book Xtreme.

**2. a.** arrive with ten big *valises* and then some. You never know what you are going to need.
  **b.** travel with two *valises*, enough to last you a week and a half.
  **c.** travel with just a *sac à dos*. You'll get what you need along the way.

**3. a.** ask if you can use *dollars*.
  **b.** exchange money at the airport and keep it in a safe place in your pants.
  **c.** exchange a bit of cash at the airport and keep your credit card handy.

**4. a.** stay at a hotel with a name in English; it's the only brand you trust.
  **b.** stay at a *petit hôtel de luxe* with the top amenities.
  **c.** stay with friends, family or in a hostel—you like to experience the city the way locals do.

**5. a.** take your most comfortable shoes, shorts and T-shirts; it's your vacation and you plan to dress like it.
  **b.** pack your most stylish clothing. You like to look your best.
  **c.** know what the locals are wearing before you go, so you don't stand out!

**6. a.** find the fast-food joints—you'll survive on burgers and fries.
  **b.** study the travel guides. They've gotta know the best places to eat, right?
  **c.** ask some locals you meet at a bar, your taxi driver, and the clerk at your hotel for recommendations.

**7. a.** are constantly asked where you're from, even before you open your mouth.
  **b.** are asked where you're from after people talk to you for a little while.
  **c.** are asked directions by other *touristes*.

**Mostly As**
  You are the tourist of all tourists, and you're not embarrassed by it. That's OK—it helps you enjoy the city comfortably. Be careful, though: you might be taken advantage of if you're not alert.

**Mostly Bs**
  You try to blend in, but you can't fool everyone. Still, you get a true taste of your vacation spot, and locals appreciate when you make an effort.

**Mostly Cs**
  You can easily pass as a local, even though you might still have an I'm-a-tourist-please-help-me moment every once in a while.

# All That Slang

*Quel temps !* So, what's the weather like while you're on your travels?

| | |
|---|---|
| **Quel temps fait-il ?** | What's the weather like? |
| **Il fait beau/froid/chaud.** | It's nice/cold/hot. |
| **Il neige.** | It's snowing. |
| **Il fait un temps de chien.** | The weather is crappy. |
| **Quel temps de merde !** 💣✳ | What shitty weather! |
| **Il fait un temps magnifique.** | The weather's perfect. |
| **Il pleut des cordes.** | It's raining cats and dogs. *Literally, it's raining ropes.* |
| **Putain, il fait chaud !** 💣✳ | It's fuckin' hot! |
| **Ça caille !** | It's freezing! |

### Know-it-all/Tout savoir

*Another way that people say "It's raining cats and dogs" is **Il pleut comme vache qui pisse**, which means it's raining like a pissing cow. We hope you have an umbrella!*

# Use It or Lose It!

Pair the pics with a caption from the word bank.

**Ça caille !**
**Il pleut des cordes.**

**Il neige.**
**Putain, il fait chaud !**

1. It's raining cats and dogs.

2. It's fuckin' hot!

3. It's freezing!

4. It's snowing.

1. Il pleut des cordes.; 2. Putain, il fait chaud !; 3. Ça caille !; 4. Il neige.

92

# All That Slang

Now that you can talk about the local weather, learn how to talk about the local food.

**J'ai un petit creux.**

I have the munchies.
*Literally, I have a little empty space.*

**On va dans un restau branché/ branchouille.**

We're going to an *in* restaurant.

**Beurk ! C'est dégueulasse ! 💣✳**

Ew! That's gross!

**Ça me donne envie de vomir.**

It makes me want to vomit.

**Miam-miam, c'est délicieux !**

Mmm, that's delicious!

**Je te ressers ?**

Can I give you seconds?

**Non merci, je suis au régime.**

No thanks, I'm on a diet.

**Non merci, j'ai les dents du fond qui baignent.**

No thanks, I'm so stuffed I could hurl.
*Literally, my back teeth are swimming.*

**Il faut que tu manges ! T'es trop maigre.**

You have to eat! You're too skinny.

**Arrête de te goinfrer, espèce de gros porc !**

Stop stuffing your face, you fat pig!

**Bon ap' !**

Bon appétit!
*The French still say **bon appétit**; use **bon ap'** with friends.*

**Ouf, j'ai trop bouffé. 💣✳**

Oof! I ate too much.
*There are two words for eating in French: **manger** and **bouffer**. The former is polite; the latter is informal.*

**Je n'ai plus faim.**

I'm full.

**Je crève la dalle !**

I'm dying of hunger!

# Use It or Lose It!

What do you say when:

1. ...something is disgusting?
2. ...something makes you want to vomit?
3. ...you're dying of hunger?
4. ...you want to say *bon appétit* to your friend?

1. Beurk ! C'est dégueulasse ! 2. Ça me donne envie de vomir. 3. Je crève la dalle ! 4. Bon ap' !

# A-List

Food you've gotta try...

1. **sandwich américain**—While this is called an American sandwich, we've certainly never seen one in the US. It's made from a baguette filled with hamburger, lettuce, tomatoes, ketchup or mayo, and fries—on top!

2. **croissants**—How can you go to France without tasting a freshly-baked croissant?

3. **baguette**—Grab one, along with a hunk of cheese and a glass of wine.

4. **saucisson**—French sausages are so yummy (insert inappropriate comment).

5. **tête de veau**—Want to try veal brain?

6. **fromage**—There are so many different types of French cheese—the smellier the better!

7. **macarons**—These little cookies are to die for.

8. **croque-monsieur**—A grilled cheese with ham and more cheese melted on top.

9. **croque-madame**—This is a **croque-monsieur** with a fried egg on top.

10. **steak-frites**—Another popular meal is steak and fries.

11. **huitres**—The French like to loosen the oyster from its shell and then slurp it up. Think jello shot with seafood.

12. **cassoulet**—This typical French dish is a bean stew usually with some kind of meat.

13. **couscous**—There's a heavy North African influence in parts of France, so find a restaurant that serves traditional **couscous**.

14. **foie gras**—Goose liver might not sound tasty, but it's one of the fanciest appetizers.

15. **crêpes**—You'll see crepe vendors in Paris just like you'll see hot dog vendors in NY.

Drinks you can't miss...

1. **vin**—You can't go to France without trying French wine. Whether it's **blanc** (white), **rosé** or **rouge** (red), you're bound to find one you like.

2. **pastis**—This is an aperitif, a drink before dinner, that tastes like licorice.

3. **diabolo menthe**—This is a mint syrup mixed with **limonade**, which is a lot like Sprite®.

4. **kir**—White wine mixed with **crème de cassis**, blackcurrant cream.

5. **coca**—Going through withdrawal? Order a **coca**, regular Coke®, or **coca light**, diet.

6. **iced tea à la pêche**—The peach-flavored iced tea is really sweet.

7. **Orangina®**—This carbonated orange juice is a favorite in France.

8. **eau-de-vie**—This "water of life" is a fruit alcohol that's enjoyed after dinner as a **digestif**.

9. **café**—After the perfect meal, try a French coffee.

10. **lait**—The French drink specially pasteurized milk, sold in non-refrigerated cartons or bottles.

# All That Slang

Get your groove on by talking about *bars* and *boîtes*.

| | |
|---|---|
| **Cette boîte est sympa.** | This club is good. |
| **Il y a un groupe différent chaque soir.** | There's a different band each night. |
| **DJ Rock est aux platines ce soir.** | DJ Rock is spinning tonight. |
| **Le cocktail de ce soir, c'est le Malibu ananas.** | Tonight's drink is the Malibu pineapple. |
| **Ce soir...** | Tonight... |
|   **2 bières pour le prix d'une.** |   beer is 2 for 1. |
|   **il y a un match de foot.** |   there's a soccer game. |
|   **il y a un groupe de rock.** |   there's a rock band. |
| **C'est la soirée spéciale filles. L'entrée est gratuite pour les filles.** | Tonight is ladies' night. Girls get in free. |
| **C'est 10 € l'entrée.** | The cover is 10 €. |
| **J'aime pas trop l'ambiance.** | I don't like the atmosphere. |
| **La boîte ferme à 2 heures.** | The club closes at 2 a.m.. |
| **C'est l'entrée VIP, ici ?** | Is this the VIP entrance? |

# Use It or Lose It!

Are you cool enough to know where each event happens?

a.

b.

c.

1. **Ce soir, il y a un match de foot.**
2. **Ce soir, il y a un groupe de rock.**
3. **C'est la soirée spéciale filles.**

1. c; 2. a; 3. b

**95**

Nice and naughty club speak…

*Tu veux danser ?*
Do you want to dance?

*Je t'offre un verre ?*
Can I buy you a drink?

*C'est un club hyper tendance.*
It's the *in* club.

*Montre-moi comment tu bouges ton cul.*
Show me how you shake that ass.

*Tu rentres avec moi si je te paie un verre ?*
Will you come home with me if I buy you a drink?

*Cette boîte est nulle à chier.*
This club fucking sucks.

Chère Vivi:
How can I find a cool French club?
Robert

Cher Robert:
The French world is full of trendy clubs and dive bars. Use common sense when trying to find the place that fits you best. Try asking young locals: *Quelle est la meilleure boîte ?* Which is the best club? Hot spots change quickly—what was in today is not in tomorrow, but these additional guidelines will help you:
  Check out the crowd, is the place full?
  How's the music?
  Do they have any good promotions like a special drink or ladies' night?
  Who's playing?
  Check the décor—if it's too tacky, run.
  Sports bars tend to be good on *foot* (soccer) nights or special events. Otherwise you'll get stuck hanging out with old dudes who don't have cable.
  If the cover is too expensive, you can be sure it's either very, very exclusive or it's a tourist trap. It might be good, but you won't get the local flavor.
    *Amuse-toi bien (Enjoy)!*
Vivi

Chère Vivi:
How old do I have to be to get into a club in France?
Anne

Chère Anne:
It all depends on the club, really. Some clubs are 16+, but most are 18+. The legal age to drink in France is 16, but you have to be 18 to drink strong liquor in a bar or club (so a beer is fine, but not a shot of vodka).
A +
Vivi

# A-List

If you're going to travel, you will need to exchange your dollars or pounds to *dollars canadiens* in Québec or *euros* in Europe.

*Argent* is the translation for money, but there are also plenty of slang terms. Here are a few. These all mean cash, although most have other meanings as well:

| | |
|---|---|
| **sous** | coins |
| **fric** | dough |
| **pognon** | loot |
| **blé** | dough *Literally, wheat* |
| **cash** | cash *You guessed it...* |
| **thune** | cash |

### Know-it-all/Tout savoir

*Even though the French switched from **francs** to **euros** in 2002, a few stores still publish their prices in euros and francs. Also, when you hear the French talk about **balles** (e.g. something costs 50 **balles**), they're referring to the price in francs and not euros.*

# ◉Dialogue: Fauché

Guillaume and Sonia are in a restaurant; they just had dinner. When *l'addition* comes, Guillaume checks his wallet...

| | | |
|---|---|---|
| GUILLAUME: | **Sonia, je suis fauché.** | Sonia, I'm broke. |
| SONIA: | **Et qu'est-ce que tu veux que je fasse ? J'ai pas mon sac.** | And what am I going to do? I don't have my purse. |
| GUILLAUME: | **Je sais pas...** | I don't know... |
| SONIA: | **T'es sûr que t'as rien ?** | Are you sure you don't have anything? |
| GUILLAUME: | **Pas un rond.** | Not a cent. |
| SONIA: | **T'es vraiment fauché.** | You're really broke. |
| GUILLAUME: | **Merde ! Il nous reste plus qu'à faire la plonge.** | Shit! We are going to have to do the dishes. |
| SONIA: | **La plonge ? Tu me prends pour qui ? Je me casse.** | The dishes! Who do you take me for? I'm leaving. |
| GUILLAUME: | **Mais...Sonia...Attends...Sonia !** | But...Sonia...Wait...Sonia! |

# Word Bytes

| | |
|---|---|
| **faire la plonge** | to do the dishes |
| | *literally, to go diving* |
| **fauché**♂/**fauchée**♀ | broke |
| **prendre** | to take |
| **sou** | cent |
| **vraiment** | really |

# 🔊 All That Slang

Broke? It's OK to admit it…

| | |
|---|---|
| **Je n'ai plus un sou/un rond.** | I don't have a penny. |
| **Je suis fauché.** | I'm broke. |
| **Il est ruiné.** | He's ruined. |
| | *This means he used to have money, but now he's broke.* |
| **Il/Elle est pauvre.** | He/She is poor. |

But if you have money…

| | |
|---|---|
| **Il est friqué** ♂/**Elle est friquée**♀. | He/She is loaded. |
| **Il est pété**♂/**Elle est pétée**♀ **de thune.** | He/She is filthy rich. |
| **Il/Elle est riche.** | He/She is rich. |
| **Il/Elle a du pognon.** | He/She has a lot of money. |

# Gesture

Does your new partner have a lot of *fric*? Rub your thumb with your index and middle finger and everyone will get the picture.

Can you accurately say if there is a lot or little cash flow?

**1.** You know that you're *ruiné*♂/*ruinée*♀ when:
    **a.** your new partner has three houses and a boat.
    **b.** your partner leaves you after cleaning out your bank account.

**2.** You know you've got some cash when:
    **a.** *Tu as du pognon.*
    **b.** *Tu n'as pas un sou.*

**3.** You know you're rich when your friends say:
    **a.** *T'es friqué*♂/*friquée*♀.
    **b.** *T'es fauché*♂/*fauchée*♀.

**4.** You've got to file for bankruptcy when:
    **a.** *Tu es riche.*
    **b.** *Tu es pauvre.*

1. b; 2. a; 3. a; 4. b

### Know-it-all/Tout savoir

When you go into a shop in France, the price you see on the tag is the price you pay. The tax, called **TVA**, is included in the price so you don't have to worry about paying extra. The same goes for restaurants. The price you see on the menu is the price you pay, including tip (it is nice to add a little extra for the tip at the end of a meal, though, if you're happy with the service). Otherwise, what you see is what you pay!

# A-List

Now that you have the cash, get some souvenirs to remember your *voyage*. While everyone loves an Eiffel Tower keychain, magnet or pencil sharpener, here are some more creative ideas of things to bring back for your friends and family:

1. A nice bottle of wine or champagne—France is known for its wine, so why not bring a bottle home for the folks?
2. If you're in the south of France, bring home some fresh lavender. Everyone loves it and your suitcase is bound to smell great.
3. How about something sweet? Get some *calissons*, a French candy, or *macarons*, a sweet pastry.
4. If you're in Paris, buy a drawing (either of yourself or of Paris) from one of the many artists around the city.
5. Paris is a very fashion-forward city, so why not think about getting some clothing or accessories for your fashion-backward friends back home?

# All That Slang

Some useful phrases when you *faites du shopping*, go shopping, and try to get a good deal.

| | |
|---|---|
| **Combien ça coûte ?** | How much does it cost? |
| **Il y a des soldes ?** | Are there sales? |
| | *There are actually only two short periods during the year when you can find sales in France: one in January and one in June.* |
| **C'est du vol.** | It's a rip-off. |
| **Je vous en donne 10 €.** | I'll give you 10 € for it. |
| **Si vous me le faites à 5 €, je vous le prends tout de suite.** | If you give it to me for 5 €, I'll take it right now. |
| **1 €, c'est mon dernier prix.** | 1 € and that's my final offer. |
| **Gardez-le, je m'en fous.** 💣* | Keep it, I don't give a damn. |
| **Vous me faites un prix, si j'en prends deux ?** | Can you give me a deal if I take two of them? |

# Use It or Lose It!

Are you ready to bargain *en français*? Match the French with the English equivalent.

1. **C'est du vol.**
2. **10 €, c'est mon dernier prix.**
3. **Gardez-le, je m'en fous.**
4. **Je vous en donne 10 €.**
5. **Si vous me le faites à 10 €, je le prends tout de suite.**

a. Keep it, I don't give a damn.
b. It's a rip-off.
c. If you give it to me for 10 €, I'll take it right now.
d. 10 €, and that's my final offer.
e. I'll give you 10 € for it.

1. b; 2. d; 3. a; 4. e; 5. c

## Know-it-all/Tout savoir

*Où est-ce que je peux acheter…?* Where can I buy…? Don't know where to get the essentials? Here's a short guide.

| | |
|---|---|
| *la bijouterie* | *jewelry store* |
| *la cordonnerie* | *shoe repair* |
| *le fleuriste* | *florist* |
| *la librairie* | *book store* |
| *le magasin d'électronique* | *electronics store* |
| *le magasin de chaussures* | *shoe store* |
| *le magasin de lingerie* | *lingerie store* |
| *le magasin de musique* | *music store* |
| *la boutique de vêtements pour femme* | *women's clothing store* |
| *la boutique de vêtements pour homme* | *men's clothing store* |
| *la boutique de vêtements/ fringues* | *clothing store* |
| *la pharmacie* | *pharmacy* |
| *la quincaillerie* | *hardware store* |
| *le supermarché* | *supermarket* |

# Use It or Lose It!

Welcome to *Xtreme Centre commercial*, the mall! With the list in hand, find the stores you need and write the name of the store next to the item. The first letter of the name of each store where you found the items will spell a secret word. Note: If you can't recognize all of the terms listed, try a dictionary!

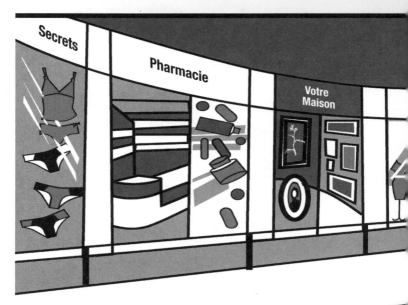

_Liste des courses_

- _tableau_
- _CD_
- _chaussures rouges à talons_
- _souvenirs_
- _boucles d'oreille_
- _jean_
- _écouteurs_
- _dessous sexy_

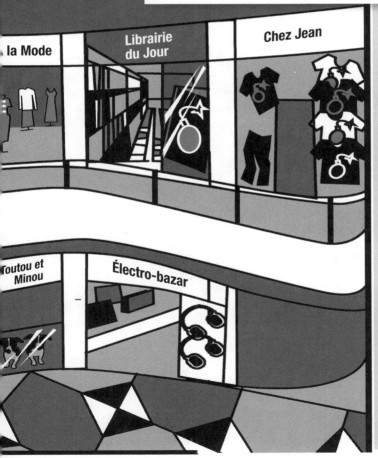

la Mode

**Librairie du Jour**

**Chez Jean**

Toutou et Minou

**Électro-bazar**

tableau=Votre Maison; CD=Audiocafé; chaussures rouges à talons=Chaussures Chaussettes; souvenirs=Attrape-Touristes; boucles d'oreille=Ninon et Fils Bijouterie; jean=Chez Jean; écouteurs (headphones)=Électro-bazar; dessous sexy (sexy underwear)=Secrets; So what was your secret word? _Vacances_, vacation, of course!

103

# Free Time

## chapter 11

## Get info on:

- the hottest French music
- four-star French films
- what's on TV
- French magazines and newspapers

## La Musique

| | | |
|---|---|---|
| DANIEL: | **Salut Julie, qu'est-ce que tu fais ?** | Hey Julie, what are you doing? |
| JULIE: | **J'écoute de la musique.** | Just listening to a little music. |
| DANIEL: | **Qu'est-ce que tu écoutes ?** | What are you listening to? |
| JULIE: | **Du hip-hop, c'est ce que je préfère.** | Hip-hop, it's my favorite kind. |
| DANIEL: | **J'aime bien ça aussi, mais je préfère le rock.** | I like it too, but I like rock better. |
| JULIE: | **Il y a un concert de Panique ce soir, on y va ?** | There's a Panique concert tonight, wanna go? |
| DANIEL: | **Pourquoi pas, mais je connais pas la musique.** | Why not, but I don't know the music. |
| JULIE: | **C'est pas grave, la musique est trop sympa et les paroles sont géniales.** | It doesn't matter, the music's great and the lyrics are awesome. |
| DANIEL: | **Est-ce que ma sœur peut venir ? Elle aussi, elle adore le hip-hop.** | Can my sister come? She loves hip-hop too. |
| JULIE: | **Bien sûr ! J'inviterai aussi les autres et on ira là-bas en groupe.** | Sure! I'll invite the others and we'll go there as a group. |
| DANIEL: | **Super, on se voit ce soir alors.** | Awesome, so I'll see you tonight. |

# Use It or Lose It!

Can you pass the polygraph? Write *vrai* if it's true and *faux* if it's not.

1. Daniel's favorite music is hip-hop.
2. Daniel and Julie are going to a concert tonight.
3. Daniel's sister loves hip-hop.
4. Panique's lyrics are great.
5. Panique is a hip-hop artist.

1. faux, Daniel prefers rock.; 2. vrai, 3. vrai, 4. vrai, 5. vrai

Chère Vivi:
What's the *in* music genre right now in France?
Merci !
Mike

Cher Mike:
There's a pretty eclectic taste in music in France. A great deal of what you hear on the radio comes directly from what's popular in the US. There's actually a French law that requires radio stations to play French-language music at least 40% of the time. That means the other 60% is usually what we hear in the Top 40 in the US.
A+,
Vivi

Chère Vivi:
What's this *tecktonik* I've heard about? How do you dance *tecktonik*?
Merci,
Pieds Gauches (Left Feet)

Chers Pieds Gauches,
*Tecktonik*, sometimes abbreviated to just TCK, is a type of dance made that came from Belgium and has quickly made its way throughout Europe and Canada. *Tecktonik* is also a fashion usually made up of funky hairstyles (think mohawk) and fluorescent, tight clothing. The dance itself is made up of different moves that involve a lot of spastic muscle movements, body contortion, pointing and basically throwing your arms all around (so make sure you're not standing close to anything fragile if you give it a shot). Go to youtube.com and type in *Tecktonik* to see some videos of people dancing. You can even find lessons where people teach you how to dance *Tecktonik*.
A+,
Vivi

# All That Slang

You need more entertainment than just music. Here's the slang on movies.

**Ce film marche très fort.**
That movie is a hit.

**Ce film est…**
That movie is…

**très marrant.**
very funny.

**hyper triste.**
really sad.

**vachement romantique.**
so romantic.

**un énorme succès.**
a blockbuster.

**nul à chier.** 💣✳
garbage.

**C'est un film à l'eau de rose.**
It's a chick flick.
*Literally, it's a rose water movie.*

**C'est trop lent, ce film. Où sont les rebondissements ?**
This movie is too slow. Where are the explosions?

**C'est quel genre de film ?**
What type of movie is it?

**C'est…**
It's…

**une comédie.**
a comedy.

**une comédie romantique.**
a romance.

**un film d'horreur.**
a horror film.

**un film dramatique.**
a drama.

**un film à suspense.**
a suspense film.

**un thriller.**
a thriller.

**un film d'action.**
an action film.

**film de cul/boules.**
a porn. *Literally, an ass/balls film.*

**J'ai trop hâte de voir ce film.**
I'm dying to see that movie.

**Je ne peux pas regarder un film sans mon pop-corn et mon coca.**
I can't watch movies without my popcorn and soda.
*You'll be asked:* **sucré ou salé**— *with sugar or salt.*

**Ferme-la, tu nous gonfles.** 💣✳
Shut up, you're pissing us off.
*For that jerk who won't let you enjoy the movie.*

If you want to bring out your inner critic, try these:

| | | |
|---|---|---|
| ★ | **Ce film est de la merde.** | This movie is shit. |
| ★ ★ | **Pas terrible.** | Not so great. |
| ★ ★ ★ | **Pas mal.** | Not bad. |
| ★ ★ ★ ★ | **Le meilleur film que j'aie jamais vu.** | The best movie I've ever seen. |

# Use It or Lose It!

Aude is a first time critic on a radio show. She's so nervous, she doesn't know what to say. Help her get her words out, in French. She thinks that:

1. The movie is slow, but it's not bad.

   _____

2. It's a chick flick, and it's funny.

   _____

3. The movie is shit.

   _____

4. There's another movie that she's dying to see.

   _____

1. C'est trop lent, ce film, mais c'est pas mal. 2. C'est un film à l'eau de rose qui est marrant. 3. Ce film est de la merde. 4. J'ai trop hâte de voir ce film.

## Quiz    Are you a movie geek?

1. When you go to the movies you buy:
   a. your *ticket*, and nothing else. You don't like being distracted.
   b. *pop-corn* and *un coca* to snack on while you enjoy the movie.
   c. an extra-large *pop-corn*, *un coca*, etc. You spend the movie throwing your snacks at people.

2. You get your *tickets*:
   a. at least one hour before the movie starts.
   b. 15 to 30 minutes before it starts, so you get in after the commercials.
   c. at least 15 minutes after the movie starts—who cares if you miss a few minutes?

3. Your favorite time to go to the movies is:
   a. if it's a great movie, you'll be at the premiere, no matter what time it is.
   b. a weekend night. It's a good way to start a long weekend.
   c. never, you'd rather rent the DVD.

4. You agree with the *critiques de films* (film critics):
   a. almost always, in fact, you send them recommendations.
   b. almost never, you loved all three Die Hards!
   c. *Critiques* ? You don't know and you don't care.

**Mostly As**
The seats at your nearest cinema have an imprint of your butt. You might want to see if you can get season tickets.

**Mostly Bs**
You like going to the movies, but you also like doing other things. Good for you.

**Mostly Cs**
You couldn't care less about movies! You've got better ways to spend your time.

# ◉All That Slang

TV lingo for couch potatoes…

| | |
|---|---|
| **Mets plus/moins fort.** | Turn up/down the volume. |
| **Qu'est-ce que tu regardes de beau ?** | What are you watching? |
| **Y a rien à regarder.** | There's nothing on. |
| **T'es un accro de la téloche.** | You're addicted to TV. |
| | *There's no expression for "couch potato" in French, but this one works well.* |
| **Je suis fan de cette émission.** | I'm a fan of this show. |
| **J'ai loupé le dernier épisode de *Plus belle la vie* hier soir.** | I missed the new episode of *Plus belle la vie* last night. |
| **Raconte-moi ce qui s'est passé.** | Tell me what happened. |
| **J'adore regarder les feuilletons.** | I love watching soaps. |

# Use It or Lose It!

What would you say if…

1. …you want to know what your friend's watching on TV?
2. …it's 2 a.m. and there are only nature shows on TV?
3. …you want to tell your friend that he's a couch potato?
4. …you're considering a 12-step plan for your addiction to soap operas?
5. …you're pissed for missing last Saturday's *Plus belle la vie* episode?
6. …you're a fan of a show?
7. …you want your friend to tell you what happened?
8. …you can't hear a thing?
9. …your ears are about to explode?

a. **Y a rien à regarder.**
b. **Mets moins fort.**
c. **J'adore regarder les feuilletons.**
d. **Qu'est-ce que tu regardes de beau ?**
e. **Je suis fan de cette émission.**
f. **J'ai loupé le dernier épisode de *Plus belle la vie*.**
g. **Raconte-moi ce qui s'est passé.**
h. **T'es un accro de la téloche.**
i. **Mets plus fort.**

1.d; 2.a; 3.h; 4.c; 5.f; 6.e; 7.g; 8.i; 9.b

## Know-it-all/Tout savoir

Ever wanted to watch French TV but figured you had to be there to see it? Not anymore. There are many different channels in France, and many of them broadcast all or some of their content directly on the web. Check out the main channels:

• TF1—www.tf1.fr
Watch the news, special reports and even French game shows like **Attention à la marche** (Watch out for the step).

• France 2—www.france2.fr
This public station has national news, special reports, movie reviews, documentaries and much more.

• France 3—www.france3.fr
This public station deals more with regional news and reports in France. There are also lots of movies and interesting political and cultural debates.

• France 5—www.france5.fr
This public station has a lot of shows on history, health, nature, art, etc.

• M6 www.m6.fr
Along with the news, you can watch different French series like **Caméra Café**, a comedy where everything takes place around the coffee machine in an office building. You can also watch some of your favorite American series in French.

# All That Slang

Talking about performance art, theater, opera, orchestra music, ballet and then some.

| | |
|---|---|
| **Tu préfères…** | You prefer… |
| **aller au théâtre.** | to go to the theater. |
| **aller à un concert.** | to go to a concert. |
| **aller à l'opéra.** | to go to the opera. |
| **aller voir un spectacle de danse.** | to go to the ballet. |
| **aller voir un spectacle.** | to see a show. |
| **aller au cirque.** | to go to the circus. |
| **aller voir une comédie musicale.** | to go to a musical. |

Everybody's a critic—here's how to talk about performances.

| | |
|---|---|
| **C'est une pièce prétentieuse qui n'a ni queue ni tête.** | It's a pretentious play that makes no sense. |
| **On m'a dit que le spectacle était génial/nul.** | They told me that the show was excellent/awful. |
| **La comédie musicale était ennuyeuse/amusante.** | The musical was boring/fun. |
| **Le chœur a très bien/mal chanté.** | The choir sang wonderfully/terribly. |
| **La danseuse est tombée—j'étais mort de rire.** | The ballerina fell—I was laughing out loud. |
| **Bof, c'était trop long.** | Eh, it was too long. |

# Use It or Lose It!

Can you pass the polygraph? Write *vrai* if it's true and *faux* if it's not.

1. If the *danseuse* was good, she was *nulle*.
2. If *l'opéra était ennuyeux*, then it was awesome.
3. You'd rather *aller à un concert* than *aller voir un spectacle*.
4. *Le concert* was good because it was *trop long*.

# Cool lit...

# Word Bytes

| | |
|---|---|
| **la BD** | comic strip *short for **bande dessinée*** |
| **le dévoreur** ♂ **/la dévoreuse** ♀ **de livres** | bookworm *literally, one who devours books* |
| **l'équilibré** ♂ **/l'équilibrée** ♀ | well-rounded |
| **le glandeur** ♂ **/la glandeuse** ♀ | slacker |
| **l'intello** | intellectual |
| **le journal** | newspaper |
| **le livre** | book |
| **le magazine** | magazine |
| **le roman** | novel |

**1.** *Tu lis* (You read):
   **a.** *tous les jours* (every day) for fun.
   **b.** *tous les jours* so that you can keep up in class discussions.
   **c.** *jamais* (never).
   **d.** *une ou deux fois par semaine* (once or twice a week).

**2.** Your favorite genre is:
   **a.** *tout* (everything).
   **b.** history, philosophy and *romans*.
   **c.** BD (but only if you're forced to read something).
   **d.** *romans policiers* (detective novels).

**3.** In a conversation about *livres*, you:
   **a.** don't really talk. That would mean you'd have to put your book down!
   **b.** dominate the conversation. You lose control when talking about books.
   **c.** are completely bored out of your mind.
   **d.** can keep up, if you feel like it.

**4.** The last thing you read was:
   **a.** Marcel Proust's *À la recherche du temps perdu* (In Search of Lost Time), some news articles, your French textbook…
   **b.** all the top books from the New York Times book review.
   **c.** *Notre-Dame de Paris*—the Cliff Notes.
   **d.** a *magazine de mode* (fashion magazine), *le journal* and half a chapter of Muriel Barbery's latest *roman*.

**Mostly As**
You are a *dévoreur♂/dévoreuse♀ de livres*. You devour books!

**Mostly Bs**
You are an *intello*. You read a lot, and you like to let people know you do.

**Mostly Cs**
You are a *glandeur♂/glandeuse♀*. You hate reading (or anything that requires energy).

**Mostly Ds**
You are *équilibré♂/équilibrée♀*, a well-rounded reader.

# A-List

Not down with literature, or even cheesy romance novels? Try comics—these and manga are big in France. There's even an international comic book festival in Angoulême where comics and *trompe-l'œil* adorn the city (*trompe-l'œil* means "to fool the eye"; these are drawings on buildings that are meant to trick you into thinking something is there when it's really not). Here are some of the most famous French or Belgian comics: *Astérix, Gaston Lagaffe, Blake & Mortimer, The Adventures of Tintin, The Adventures of Nero, The Smurfs, Titeuf*

# Bad Language

**chapter 12**

## Get info on:

- cursing
- how to know you've been insulted
- how to fight back
- how to get away with cursing

## DISCLAIMER

We don't recommend using these words and expressions but in case you overhear them, we want you to know what people are saying! We are not responsible if you get a black eye or a rearranged smile from using these insults. Warning! There are no ●✱●✱ in this chapter, because all the language is bad!

## A-List: Top *jurons*

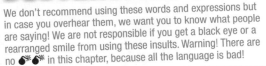

| | |
|---|---|
| **merde** | shit *You can also insert …**de merde** after any noun to make the noun shitty. For example, **mon travail de merde** means my shitty job.* |
| **putain** | fuck |
| **Putain de merde !** | Fucking shit! |
| **Putain de bordel de merde !** | Fucking whorehouse of shit! *Pretty much one of the worst things one can say in French.* |
| **con** | idiot *Literally, this means cunt, but it's used to say someone is stupid.* |
| **connard**♂ | asshole, dumb ass |
| **pétasse**♀**/salope**♀ | bitch/slut |
| **pute**♀ | whore |
| **salaud**♂ | bastard, scumbag |
| **J'en ai rien à foutre.** | I don't give a shit. |
| **fils de pute**♂ | son of a bitch |
| **Va te faire foutre !** | Go fuck yourself! *Literally, Go get yourself fucked!* |
| **Casse-toi !** | Fuck off! |
| **Ta gueule !** | Shut the fuck up! |
| **Nique ta mère !** | Fuck your mom! ***Ta mère** is just as effective.* |

**113**

# Use It or Lose It!

Meet Joe W., the biggest *connard*, asshole, ever. Look at the things people have said about him, and see if you can describe him in English. Write the translation next to the French.

MEET JOE W.

1. He's *un fils de pute*.

2. His favorite curse word is *putain*.

3. He's *un salaud*.

4. He's such a *connard*.

5. He's full of *merde*.

1. a son of a bitch
2. fuck
3. a bastard
4. asshole
5. shit

### Know-it-all/Tout savoir

If you were to learn only one curse word, it should be *putain* thanks to its sheer versatility. Exclaim it once and it means "Fuck!" Say it more calmly and it can mean "Wow! or "Holy shit!" Call a woman a *pute* (the shortened version) and it means she's a whore. Call a guy a *fils de pute* and he's the son of a whore. Call anything a *putain de* (something) and it means a fucking (something).

Chère Vivi
My French-speaking friends are major guttermouths. Are there any more nasty words I should know?
Yours,
Patty Mousse

Chère Patty:
These are the *jurons* that did not make the countdown...

**connasse** ♀
It's used like *salope* and *pétasse* to mean bitch/slut.

**enfoiré** ♂
This is another way of saying *salaud* or bastard.

**Va te faire voir !**
This is another way to say go fuck yourself, but it literally means go

make yourself be seen. Why is that an insult? Who knows.

**Va te faire enculer !**
Go fuck yourself in the ass!

**tabernac**
This is one of the worst curses you can use in Canada, used kind of like *putain*.

**J'en ai rien à branler.**
Literally, this means I have nothing to jerk off, but it's another way of saying I don't give a shit.

**pauvre con** ♂
Literally this means poor cunt, but it's a way of calling someone a jerk.

**trou du cul/trouduc**
These literally mean asshole.

# Use It or Lose It!

Fill in the correct usage of *putain* for each picture.

a. **Pute !**

b. **Fils de pute !**

c. **Putain de porte !**

1. a; 2. b; 3. c.

# Use It or Lose It!

What would you say to Philippe in the following circumstances?

1. Philippe just said to you: *Va te faire foutre*.
2. Philippe just dumped his girlfriend while they were having sex.
3. Philippe is selling himself cheap on the streets.

a. **Va te faire enculer, pauvre con !**
b. **Pute !**
c. **Enfoiré !**

1. a; 2. c; 3. b.

# Use It or Lose It!

What did that potty mouth just say? Complete the naughty expressions.

a. **T'es un** _____ .

b. _____ **ta mère !**

c. **Va te faire** _____ .

d. **J'en ai rien à** _____ .

e. _____ **! Je ne veux plus te voir (I don't want to see you anymore) !**

a. connard, enfoiré, pauvre con, trou du cul, etc.; b. Nique, voir, foutre, enculer; c. foutre, voir, foutre, branler; e. Casse-toi

# 🔊 Les femmes bien élevées ne devraient pas jurer ?

Well mannered ladies shouldn't curse?

# Use It or Lose It!

Can you remember what these words mean?

a. connard

b. salope

c. pute

d. con

## Q&A

**Chère Vivi**
I've heard the expression *sacrebleu* used before, but I don't get it. Someone told me it translates to "sacred blue", but what's so vulgar about that?

Yours,
Christian

**Cher Christian:**
We've all heard *sacrebleu* before (think cartoons), but most people don't know what it means or where it comes from. It's a heavily outdated way to say "Gee!", and you'll get some strange looks if you say it in France.

Vivi

Innocent "curses" and the not-so-innocent...

*Punaise!*
Push-pin!

*This is like saying gosh darn it instead of God damn it.*

*Mince!*
Shoot!

*Il est gonflé.♂/Elle est gonflée.♀*
He/She has some nerve.

*Zut!*
Darn!

*Laisse-moi tranquille.*
Leave me alone.

*Ça m'est égal.*
I don't care.

*Je m'en contrefous!*
I don't give a flying fuck!

*Putain, fais chier!*
Fucking shit!

*Literally, Whore, [you] make me take a shit!*

*Nique ta mère.*
Go fuck your mother.

*Quel enfoiré de merde.♂*
What a fucking bastard.

*Va chier.*
Go fuck yourself.

*Literally, Go shit.*

117

# Quiz How dirty are you?

For each situation, choose one way of responding. You will get points depending on how you respond—the dirtier, the better.

1. Your teacher just handed back your paper on how to make the world *écologique*. You got a crappy score with a frowning face (your teacher has a childish sense of humor). Meanwhile, your best friends are very excited because they all got high marks (and a smiley), and one of them comes over to tell you. You say:
   a. *Ça m'est égal.*
   b. *Je m'en contrefous.*

2. Someone just cut you off while you were driving. He gives you the finger, and you almost hit another car. You scream:
   a. *Il est gonflé!*
   b. *Quel enfoiré de merde!*

3. You just spilled a whole cup of hot coffee on your new *ordinateur portable*. You shout:
   a. *Putain, fait chier!*
   b. *Punaise!*

4. Your ex wants you back, even though the *connard ♂/connasse ♀* cheated on you with your best friend. You say:
   a. *Nique ta mère!*
   b. *Laisse-moi tranquille.*

5. You stubbed your toe on the corner of your desk. It hurts like a bitch and you shout:
   a. *Aïe!*
   b. *Putain!*

# All That Slang

A course in curse… Learn the proper ways to be improper.

| | |
|---|---|
| **Putain, j'ai pas de bol !** | I have no fucking luck! |
| **Tu m'emmerdes.** | You're pissing me off. |
| **Va te branler.** | Go fuck yourself. *Literally, go jerk off.* |
| **Va te faire voir, pauvre conne. ♀** | Go fuck yourself, you dumb bitch. |
| **Va te faire mettre, pauvre con. ♂** | Go fuck yourself, dumbass. |
| **Va te faire enculer.** | Fuck off. *Literally, Go get yourself fucked in the ass.* |
| **Lui, c'est une tête de nœud.** | That guy's a dickhead. |
| **M. Smith est un fils de pute.** | Mr. Smith is a son of a bitch. |
| **J'ai foiré mon examen de français.** | I fucked up on my French test. |
| **Lui, c'est un loser.** | He's such a loser/fuck-up. |
| **Ce match de foot était de la merde.** | That soccer game was shit. |
| **C'est un bon coup.** | He/She's a good fuck. |
| **J'ai niqué ma bagnole.** | I fucked up my car. |
| **C'est rien que de la merde.** | It's just a bunch of shit. |
| **Je n'y crois pas à tes conneries.** | I'm not believing any of your bullshit. |
| **Ne joue pas au con avec moi.** | Don't mess with me. |
| **Va te faire voir chez les Grecs.** | Go fuck yourself. *Literally, Go make yourself seen at the Greeks.* |

# Use It or Lose It!

Paul received this *courriel* from his friend Dale, but the curses are missing! Can you help him turn this into an R-rated email?

---

Hey _____ (asshole) 💣✳

_____ ! (Fucking shit!) We lost the _____ (fucking) soccer game

because the _____ (stupid asshole) referee is blind. I told that _____

(loser) "_____" (go fuck yourself) and he kicked me out of the game. Can

you believe that _____ (jerk)? _____ (I have no fucking luck).

Dale

---

# ● Dialogue: The interview

Susan is a new reporter for the network FrancoMonde. Her first assignment is to interview Marc Lebeau, a new French heartthrob. Unfortunately, he is in a bad mood...

SUSAN: **Marc Lebeau, j'ai entendu dire que vous aviez une nouvelle amoureuse.**

Marc Lebeau, I heard that you have a new lover.

MARC LEBEAU: **Qu'est-ce que ça peut vous foutre ?**

What the fuck does it matter to you?

SUSAN: **Alors, ce n'est pas vrai ?** (confused)

So, it's not true?

MARC LEBEAU: **Putain, ça vous regarde pas.**

It's none of your fucking business.

SUSAN: **Mais, Marc Lebeau, c'est pas grave.**

But, Marc Lebeau, it's no big deal.

MARC LEBEAU: **Ah bon ? J'en ai marre qu'on me pose les mêmes putain de questions.**

Really? I'm tired of being asked the same fucking question.

SUSAN: **Bon ben, désolée... changeons de sujet.**

Well sorry... let's change the subject.

MARC LEBEAU: **Bonne idée.**

Good idea.

SUSAN: **Voulez-vous dire un petit mot à vos fans ?**

Do you want to say a little something to your fans?

MARC LEBEAU: **Oui, je les adore, même s'ils sont tous des pauvres cons ! Ciao, salope !**

Yes, that I love them, even if they're all dumbasses! Ciao bitch!

SUSAN: **Vous êtes vraiment grossier !**

You're a real potty mouth!

# Word Bytes

| | |
|---|---|
| **Qu'est-ce que ça peut vous foutre ?** | What the fuck does it matter to you? |
| **Putain, ça vous regarde pas.** | It's none of your fucking business. |
| **C'est pas grave.** | It's no big deal. |
| **Vous êtes vraiment grossier !** | You're a real potty mouth! |

# Use It or Lose It!

Susan's interview was censored by FrancoMonde (what a surprise!). Exchange the *bips* with Marc Lebeau's curses.

SUSAN: **Marc Lebeau, j'ai entendu dire que vous aviez une nouvelle amoureuse.**

MARC LEBEAU: **Qu'est-ce que ça peut vous –bip- ?**

SUSAN: **Alors, ce n'est pas vrai ?**

MARC LEBEAU: **-Bip-, ça vous regarde pas.**

SUSAN: **Mais, Marc Lebeau, c'est pas grave.**

MARC LEBEAU: **Ah bon? J'en ai –bip- qu'on me pose les mêmes –bip- questions.**

SUSAN: **Bon ben, désolée… changeons de sujet.**

MARC LEBEAU: **Bonne idée.**

SUSAN: **Voulez-vous dire un petit mot à vos fans ?**

MARC LEBEAU: **Oui, je les adore, même s'ils sont tous des –bip- ! Ciao –bip- !**

foutre, putain, marre, putain de, pauvres cons, salope

# Use It or Lose It!

Think of this as the R-rated version of the Sunday crossword puzzle.

**Across**

3 son of a bitch
6 se _____ (to jerk off)
8 Va te faire _____
9 Ta _____! (Shut up!)
12 asshole
13 Va te faire _____.
16 Putain de _____ de merde!
17 Va _____ ta mère.

**Down**

1 dickhead
2 Putain, fais _____.
4 a Canadian curse word
5 bastard
7 whore
10 Va te faire _____.
11 Ce mec est _____ (nuts).
14 slut
15 Darn!

Across: 3. filsdepute; 6. branler; 8. foutre; 9. gueule; 12. connard; 13. voir; 16. bordel; 17. niquer
Down: 1. têtedenoeud; 2. chier; 4. tabernac; 5. salaud; 7. putain; 10. enculer; 11. barjot; 14. salope; 15. zut

# Anti-dictionary

You're not gonna find the typical terms in this dictionary, but you will find all of the cool terms, slanguage and swear words used in this book, and then some. Other things you should note:

- Who says a dictionary has gotta be A to Z? This one is Z to A!
- Don't know if a noun is feminine or masculine? If it says *le* it's masculine, *la* it's feminine. If it starts with a vowel or if it's plural, look for ♂/♀.
- Look for ♂/♀ to figure out how to gender-bend adjectives.

**zit**      le bouton 78, 80

**zipper**      la braguette 71

**you**      tu (informal) 20, 26, 32, 34, 36, 37, 42, 44, 47, 49, 51, 53, 63, 66, 68, 72, 74, 76, 77, 78, 81, 82, 93, 96, 99, 104, 106, 108, 110, 112, 119, vous (formal) 19, 26, 49, 81, 88, 100, 12

**yesterday**      hier 79, 108

**yeah right**      c'est ça 60

**wrinkle**      la ride 77, 78

**with**      avec 34, 36, 44, 47, 60, 63, 65, 68, 71, 72, 84, 86, 88, 96, 119

**wireless**      sans fil 66

**wine**      le vin 16, 17, 87, 94

| | |
|---|---|
| **window** | la fenêtre 75, 76 |
| **wife** | la femme 24 |
| **why** | pourquoi 34, 41, 53, 104 |
| **whore** | la pute ●* 68, 71, 113, 114, 115, 117, 119 |
| **who** | qui 20, 21, 23, 29, 30, 44, 71, 76, 79, 80, 81, 92, 93, 97, 107, 108, 110 |
| **white wine** | le vin blanc 94 |
| **what** | que (relative pronoun) 21, 31, 34, 35, 36, 37, 49, 51, 52, 53, 56, 57, 63, 66, 69, 71, 74, 77, 80, 82, 88, 93, 97, 101, 104, 106, 108, 110, 119, 120, 121, quoi (as a question or exclamation) 7, 11, 12, 13, 20, 22, 23, 29, 30, 32, 35, 36, 47, 52, 53, 60, 71 |
| **website** | le site Web 47, 48, 49 |
| **weather** | le temps 92, 112 |
| **we** | nous 85, 97, 106 |
| **water** | l'eau ♀ 81, 94, 106, 107 |
| **watch** | la montre 70 |
| **want, to** | vouloir 23, 34, 35, 36, 44, 49, 74, 77, 78, 96, 97, 116, 120, 121 |
| **wall** | le mur 53, 75 |

| | |
|---|---|
| **vomit, to** | vomir (standard) 79, 93, dégueuler (slang) 11, 79 |
| **virgin** | vierge 45 |
| **view** | la vue 88, 89 |
| **videogame console** | la console de jeux 61 |

| | |
|---|---|
| **videogame** | le jeu vidéo 61 |
| **versatile** | versatile 31 |
| **vagina** | la chatte (slang) 38, la foufoune (slang, genitalia) ●* 38 |
| **vacation** | les vacances (always plural) ♀ 84, 103 |

| | |
|---|---|
| **use, to** | utiliser 44 |
| **upload, to** | mettre en ligne (a video) 56, 57 |
| **undress, to** | se mettre à poil (slang) 39, 40 |

| they | ils ♂/elles ♀ 31, 43, 73 |
| --- | --- |
| thanks | merci 12, 13, 19, 54, 62, 81, 83, 90, 93, 105 |
| text, to | envoyer un SMS 49 |
| testicles | les burnes ♀ (slang) 38, les couilles ♀ (slang) 38 |
| tell, to | dire 10, 20, 21, 29, 30, 81, 88, 118, 120, 121, raconter 108 |
| taste | le goût 75, 76 |
| tan, to | se faire bronzer 84 |
| take care of, to | prendre soin de 23 |
| tacky | kitsch 74, 75 |
| table | la table 75, 76 |

| sweetie | chouchou 18, 20, ma puce 18 |
| --- | --- |

| suspense | le suspense 106 |
| --- | --- |

| surf (the net), to | surfer sur le net 49 |
| --- | --- |
| sure | sûr ♂/sûre ♀ 97 |
| supermarket | le supermarché 82, 101 |
| sunglasses | les lunettes ♀ de soleil 70 |
| suck, to | sucer 39 |
| stress | le stress 77, 78 |
| stovetop | la cuisinière 75 |
| story | l'histoire ♀ 20 |
| store | le magasin 101 |
| STD | la MST (Maladie Sexuellement Transmissible) 79 |
| stand, to | supporter (to put up with) 23 |
| spinster | la vieille fille 15, 16, 23 |

| speaker | l'enceinte ♀ 61, 62 |
| --- | --- |
| sorry | désolé ♂/désolée ♀ 10, 66, 120, 121 |
| son of a bitch | le fils de pute 💣✳ 113, 114, 115, 119 |

| | |
|---|---|
| **see, to** | voir 34, 35, 63, 85, 86, 106, 107, 110, 116 |
| **search, to** | chercher 34, 35, 36, 42, 43, 52, rechercher 49, 50, 54, 55, 56, 65, 112 |
| **sea** | la mer 88, 89 |
| **screwed, to be** | être foutu ♂ /foutue ♀ 36, 82 |
| **save, to** | sauvegarder (tech term) 50 |
| **sales** | les soldes ♀ 100 |
| **sad** | triste 106 |
| **s.o.b.** | fils de pute ●※ 113, 114, 115, 119 |

| | |
|---|---|
| **rub, to** | frotter 39 |
| **rosé wine** | le rosé 94 |
| **room** | la chambre (bedroom) 74, 75, 76, 88, 89, 90, la salle (other room) 75, 88, 89 |
| **romantic** | romantique 106 |
| **romance** | la comédie romantique (movie) 106 |
| **rock** | le rock (music) 95, 104, 105 |
| **ring** | la bague 70 |
| **right now** | maintenant 49, 78, 79 |

| | |
|---|---|
| **ridiculous** | ridicule 23, 71, 73 |
| **rich, to be** | être riche (standard) 98, 99, être friqué ♂ /friquée ♀ (slang) 98, 99, avoir du pognon (slang) 97, 98, 99 |

| | |
|---|---|
| **reuse, to** | réutiliser 81, 82 |
| **restart, to** | redémarrer 66 |
| **reply, to** | répondre 47, 48 |
| **rental** | la location 88, 89, 90 |
| **remember, to** | se souvenir 84 |
| **relax, to** | se décontracter 37, 77, 78 |
| **red wine** | le vin rouge 16, 17, 94 |
| **ready** | prêt ♂ /prête ♀ 35 |

| | |
|---|---|
| **question** | la question 88, 89 |

| | |
|---|---|
| **pussy** | la chatte (slang) (both the female cat and the vagina) 38, la foufoune (slang) 38 |

| | |
|---|---|
| **purse** | le sac à main 90 |
| **program** | l'émission (TV) 65, 108, le logiciel (computer) 49, 51 |
| **profile** | le profil 47, 53, 54, 59, 64, 65 |
| **printer** | l'imprimante ♀ 61 |

| | |
|---|---|
| **print, to** | imprimer 48, 49, 60 |
| **potty mouth, to have a** | être grossier ♂/grossière ♀ 120 |
| **porn movie** | le film de cul (slang) 106 |
| **popcorn** | le pop-corn 106, 107 |
| **poor** | pauvre 98, 99, fauché ♂/ fauchée ♀ (broke) 97, 98, 99 |
| **pool** | la piscine 76, 84, 88, 89, 90 |
| **pleasure** | le plaisir 44 |
| **play** | la pièce (theater) 110 |
| **planner** | l'agenda ♂ 67 |
| **pinch, to** | pincer 45 |
| **pillow** | l'oreiller ♂ 75, 76 |
| **picture** | la photo 53, 60, 61, 63, 65, 67, 84 |
| **phone call** | l'appel ♂ 64, le coup de fil 35, 66 |
| **pharmacy** | la pharmacie 101, 102 |

| | |
|---|---|
| **personality** | la personnalité 16, 17 |
| **penis** | la bite ♦✳ 38, la queue (slang) ♦✳ 38 |
| **pee, to** | pisser ♦✳ 79, 92 |
| **password** | le mot de passe 47, 48, 49, 50 |
| **party animal** | le fêtard/la fêtarde 15, 16, 17, 22, 26 |
| **party** | la fête 13, 16, 17, 87 |

| | |
|---|---|
| **partner** | le/la partenaire 40, 45 |

| | |
|---|---|
| **panty** | la culotte 69, 70 |

| | |
|---|---|
| **pants** | le pantalon 68, 70, 71, 72, 73 |

| | |
|---|---|
| **painting** | le tableau (on display) 74, 75, 76, 103 |
| **package** | le paquet 38 |

| | |
|---|---|
| **oven** | le four 75 |
| **outfit** | la tenue 33, 69, 70, 71, 72 |
| **ouch** | aïe 23, 116, 118 |
| **online** | en ligne 47, 48, 49, 56, 57 |
| **old-fashioned** | vieux jeu 23, 51 |
| **OK** | d'accord 35, 51, OK 53 |
| **offended** | offensé ♂/offensée ♀ 9 |

| | |
|---|---|
| **nudist** | le/la nudiste 86 |
| **novel** | le roman 111, 112 |
| **nose** | le nez 79 |
| **no big deal** | pas grave 45, 104, 120, 121 |
| **nice** | sympa 7, 10, 16, 17, 34, 49, 85, 95, 104 |
| **newspaper** | le journal 111, 112 |
| **never** | jamais 20, 23, 106, 112 |
| **network** | le réseau 49, 53, 54, 63, 66 |
| **nervous** | nerveux ♂/nerveuse ♀ 37 |

**130**

| | |
|---|---|
| **nerd** | le nerd 59 |
| **neighbor** | le voisin/la voisine 20, 22 |
| **necklace** | le collier 70 |

| | |
|---|---|
| **music** | la musique 16, 17, 53, 65, 67, 87, 101, 104 |
| **museum** | le musée 85, 86 |
| **muscle** | le muscle 78 |
| **MP3 player** | le lecteur MP3 60, 61, 63 |

| | |
|---|---|
| **movie** | le film 13, 65, 86, 88, 89, 90, 106 |
| **move, to** | bouger 96 |
| **mouse** | la souris (animal and technological) 61, 62, 66 |
| **motherfucker** | l'enfoiré ♂/l'enfoirée ♀ de merde ●ᵂ 118 |

| | |
|---|---|
| **money** | l'argent ♂ (standard) 97, le pognon (slang) 97, 98, 99, le blé (slang) 97, la thune (slang) 97, 98, le cash (slang) 97, le fric (slang) 97, 98 |
| **mom** | la mère 23, 113, 116, 117, 118, 122, la maman 23, 24, 25, 71 |

| | |
|---|---|
| **mirror** | le miroir 74, 75, 76, la glace 71, 73 |
| **microwave** | le micro-ondes 67, 75 |
| **mess** | le bordel (literally, a brothel) 20, 21, 22 |
| **me** | moi 22, 23, 34, 35, 42, 47, 66, 74, 96, 108, 117, 118, 119 |
| **masturbate, to** | se masturber (standard) 39, se branler (slang) 39, 122 |

| | |
|---|---|
| **marry, to** | se marier 23 |

| | |
|---|---|
| **many** | beaucoup de 16, 44, 82 |
| **make, to** | faire 39, 44, 45, 53, 60, 74, 79 |
| **make love, to** | faire l'amour (standard) 39, 43, 45, baiser (slang) 💣❋ 36, 37, 39, 42, 43, 44 |
| **magazine** | le magazine 111, 112 |

| | |
|---|---|
| **lyrics** | les paroles ♀ 104 |
| **luggage** | les bagages ♂ 90 |
| **luck** | la chance 32, 37, 54, 62 |
| **lover** | l'amant ♂ 43 |
| **love, to** | aimer 31, 33, 41, 42, 43, 52, 53, 74, 85 |

| | |
|---|---|
| **love** | l'amour ♂ 39, 43, 45, les amours ♀ 80 |

| | |
|---|---|
| **loudspeaker** | le haut-parleur 64 |
| **loogey** | le crachat 79 |
| **LOL** | MDR (mort de rire) 52 |
| **log out, to** | se déconnecter 49 |
| **log in, to** | se connecter 63 |
| **listen, to** | écouter 34, 53, 104 |

| | |
|---|---|
| **liquor** | l'alcool ♂ 16, 17 |

| | |
|---|---|
| **link** | le lien 47, 48, 49, 50, 51 |
| **lingerie** | la lingerie 101 |

| | |
|---|---|
| **like, to** | aimer bien 42, 43, 74, 104 |
| **life** | la vie 33, 94 |

| | |
|---|---|
| **lie, to** | mentir 20 |
| **lie down, to** | s'allonger 78 |
| **lick, to** | lécher 40 |
| **less** | moins 52, 108 |
| **lesbian** | la lesbienne (standard) 27, la gouine (slang) 💣✳ 27, 28, 29, la goudou (slang) 💣✳ 27, la broute-gazon (slang) 💣✳ 27 |

| | |
|---|---|
| **lecture** | la conférence 88, 89 |
| **leave, to** | se casser (slang) 41, 42, 43, 97 |
| **laugh, to** | rire 52, 110 |
| **lamp** | la lampe 75 |
| **ladies' night** | la soirée spéciale filles 95 |

| | |
|---|---|
| **kitchen** | la cuisine 74, 75 |

| | |
|---|---|
| **husband** | le mari 24 |
| **hurt** | blessé ♂ /blessée ♀ 33 |
| **how** | comment (as a question or exclamation) 20, 36, 56, 57, 72, 96 |
| **hottie** | beau gosse ♂ 14, 17, super nana ♀ 14, 16, 17 |

| | |
|---|---|
| **hotel** | l'hôtel ♂ 85, 86, 88, 89, 90, 91 |
| **hot** | chaud ♂ , chaude ♀ 81, 82, 92 |
| **horror** | l'horreur ♀ 106 |
| **horrible** | horrible 71, 73 |
| **horoscope** | l'horoscope ♂ 44 |
| **horny** | chaud ♂ /chaude ♀ 52 |
| **home** | la maison 12, 13, 74, 75 |
| **hit on, to** | draguer 36, 37 |
| **hit** | un succès (as in movie blockbuster) 106 |
| **high heel (shoe)** | le talon haut 70, 72 |

| | |
|---|---|
| **hello** | bonjour (standard) 62, 74, salut (informal) 10, 34, 36, 37, 47, 50, 53, 55, 63, 104, allô (on the phone) 50, 63 |
| **hear, to** | entendre 21, 63, 120, 121 |
| **headphones** | le casque 61, 62, les écouteurs ♂ 61, 103 |
| **head** | la tête 79, 94, 119, 122 |
| **he** | il 22, 31, 33, 41, 42, 43, 47, 55, 71, 79, 88, 98, 117, 118 |
| **have, to** | avoir 76, 98, 99 |
| **hate, to** | détester 42, 43, 79, 81, haïr 41, 42 |
| **hardware store** | la quincaillerie 101 |
| **happen, to** | se passer 21, 22, 108 |
| **hangover** | la gueule de bois 79 |

| | |
|---|---|
| **handsome** | beau ♂ /belle ♀ 69 |
| **hand luggage** | les bagages ♂ à main 90 |
| **hand job** | la branlette 39 |
| **hand** | la main 90 |
| **hair** | les cheveux ♂ 35 |

| | |
|---|---|
| **hack, to** | pirater 49 |

| | |
|---|---|
| **guy** | le mec 14, 17, 31, 41, 42, 47, 55, 67, 88, 89, 119, 122, le type 14, le keum (verlan) 14 |

| | |
|---|---|
| **green, to be** | être écolo 81, 83 |
| **great** | génial ♂/géniale ♀ 7, 8, 9, 10, 12, 13, 23, 34, 36, 47, 85, 104, 110, magnifique 71, 74, 92 |
| **grandpa** | le grand-père (standard) 26, pépé (informal) 23, 24, 26 |
| **grandma** | la grand-mère (standard) 26, mémé (informal) 16, 17, 23, 24, 25, 26 |
| **gothic** | gothique 23 |

| | |
|---|---|
| **gossip, to** | cancaner 20 |
| **gossip** | la commère (person) 20, le potin (info) 20, 21 |
| **gorgeous** | magnifique 71, 92 |
| **go out, to** | sortir 29, 30, 35, 36, 42, 43, 44, 54, 69, 79 |
| **go on a cruise, to** | faire une croisière 84, 86 |
| **glasses** | les lunettes 23 |
| **give, to** | donner 56, 57, 77, 78, 100, 101 |
| **girlfriend** | la copine 16, 17, 20, 42 |
| **girl** | la fille (standard) 47, 55, 95, la nana (informal) 14, 16, 17, 67, la meuf (verlan) 14, 15 |

| | |
|---|---|
| **get lost, to** | se perdre (standard) 50, 56, 112, se paumer (slang) 85 |
| **genre** | le genre 65, 105, 106, 112 |
| **gay (person)** | le gay 27, 28, 30, l'homo (standard) 27, le pédé 💣✳ 27, la pédale 💣✳ 27 |

| | |
|---|---|
| **drag queen** | la/le drag-queen 27, 31 |
| **download, to** | télécharger 49, 50, 51, 66 |
| **door** | la porte 75, 115 |
| **dollar** | le dollar 91, 97 |
| **document** | le document 50 |
| **do, to** | faire 34, 35, 36, 37, 53, 60, 74, 77, 78, 82, 104 |
| **disgusting** | dégueulasse ●※ 11, 93 |
| **digital camera** | l'appareil photo numérique ♂ 60, 61 |

| | |
|---|---|
| **diet, to be on a** | être au régime 93 |
| **diarrhea, to have** | avoir la chiasse ●※ 79, 80 |
| **delicious** | délicieux ♂/délicieuse ♀ 93 |

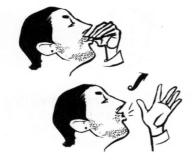

| | |
|---|---|
| **delete, to** | supprimer 48 |
| **decorate, to** | décorer 75 |

| | |
|---|---|
| **dear** | cher ♂/chère ♀ 9, 19, 26, 32, 37, 54, 62, 90, 96, 105, 115, 117 |
| **day** | le jour 83, 103, 112, la journée 85 |
| **date** | le rendez-vous 34, 36, 37, 47 |
| **darling** | chéri ♂/chérie ♀ 18, 20, 81 |
| **dance, to** | danser 96 |
| **dance** | la danse 16, 17, 110 |
| **dad** | le papa 23, 24, 25 |

## C

| | |
|---|---|
| **curtain** | le rideau 75, 76 |
| **curse** | le juron 113, 115 |
| **cunt** | la chatte ●※ 38, la foufoune ●※ 38, le con ●※ (body part) 11, l'espèce de conne ♀, la connasse (person) ●※ 42, 115, 118 |
| **cruise** | la croisière 84, 86 |
| **critic** | le/la critique 107 |
| **crazy** | fou ♂/folle ♀ 77, 78 |
| **cousin** | le cousin/la cousine 23 |
| **corner** | le coin 12, 13 |
| **cop** | le flic 15, le keuf (verlan) 15 |

| | |
|---|---|
| **cool** | cool 9, 10, 13, 23, 47, |
| **(exclama-** | 51, 111, sympa 7, 10, |
| **tion or** | 17, 34, 49, 95, 104, |
| **state of** | excellent♂/excellente♀ |
| **being)** | 8, 13, super 7, 8, 10, 36, |
| | 104, génial♂/géniale♀ |
| | 7, 8, 9, 10, 12, 13, 23, |
| | 34, 36, 47, 85, 104, 110, |
| | top 8, trop fort 8, 9, 12, |
| | 13, ça déchire 7, 8, 9, |
| | 10, ça pète 8, 9, 10, 12, |
| | 13, c'est de la balle 8, |
| | trop classe 7 |
| **connect, to** | se connecter 63 |
| **condom** | la capote (informal) 44, |
| | 79, 80 |
| **concert** | le concert 104, 110 |
| **computer** | l'ordinateur♂ (standard) |
| | 61, 62, 67, 118, l'ordi |
| | (informal) 49, 61, 66, 67 |

| | |
|---|---|
| **comic strip** | la bande dessinée 8, 111, |
| | la BD 8, 111, 112 |
| **comfortable** | confortable (only for things) |
| | 74, 78 |
| **comedy** | la comédie 106, 110 |
| **come, to** | venir 34, 35, 36, 104, jouir |
| | (sexual) 39 |

| | |
|---|---|
| **color** | la couleur 44, 45, 74, 75 |
| **college** | l'université♀ 77, la fac |
| | (informal) 77, 78 |
| **cold** | froid♂/froide♀ 7, 85, 92 |
| **coffee** | le café 16, 87, 94 |
| **cock** | la bite ✹* 38, la queue |
| | ✹* 38 |
| **coat** | le manteau 70, 72 |
| **club** | la boîte (place) 31, 72, |
| | 95, 96 |
| **clothes** | les vêtements♂ (standard) |
| | 72, 101, les fringues♀ |
| | (slang) 81, 101 |
| **closet** | le placard 29, 30, 32, 33, |
| | 75 |
| **close, to** | fermer 50, 95 |
| **clock** | l'horloge♀ 47, 65 |
| **click, to** | cliquer 48, 49, 58 |

| | |
|---|---|
| **circus** | le cirque 110 |
| **cheat, to** | tromper (someone) 45 |
| **chat, to** | chatter (online) 47, 48, 49, |
| | 51, 52, 53 |
| **change, to** | changer 63, 74, 75, 120, |
| | 121 |

| | |
|---|---|
| **chandelier** | le lustre 75 |
| **chair** | la chaise 75 |
| **center** | le centre 88, 89, 90 |
| **cell phone** | le portable 61, 62, 63, 65, 66, 67, 88, 89, 90, le cellulaire (Canada) 61, 62, le natel (Switzerland) 61, 62 |

| | |
|---|---|
| **ceiling** | le plafond 74, 75 |
| **carpool** | le covoiturage 82 |
| **car** | la voiture (standard) 8, 11, 22, 82, 83, la bagnole (slang) 119 |
| **candle** | la bougie 75 |
| **cancel, to** | annuler 64 |
| **camping, to go** | faire du camping 72 |
| **call, to** | appeler 64, 65 |

| | |
|---|---|
| **buy, to** | acheter 49, 52, 63, 101 |
| **button** | le bouton 49, 64, 65 |

| | |
|---|---|
| **butt cheek** | la fesse 8, 38, 71, 73 |
| **butt** | le cul (slang) 36, 38, 44, 45, 79, 96, 106, 115, 116, 119 |
| **but** | mais 44, 45, 49, 51, 60, 66, 68, 69, 85, 97, 104, 107, 121 |

| | |
|---|---|
| **busy** | occupé ♂/occupée ♀ 35, 52 |
| **brother** | le frère (standard) 20, 23, le frangin (informal) 24, 25, 26 |
| **broke, to be** | être fauché ♂/fauchée ♀ 97, 98, 99, être ruiné ♂/ruinée ♀ 98, 99 |
| **bracelet** | le bracelet 70 |
| **bra** | le soutien-gorge 69, 70 |
| **boyfriend** | le copain 16, 17, 20, 42, 85, 86 |
| **boy** | le garçon 33, le gamin 24 |
| **bottom** | passif (for gay men) 31 |
| **boring** | ennuyeux ♂/ennuyeuse ♀ 110 |

| | |
|---|---|
| boot | la botte 70 |
| bookworm | le dévoreur♂/la dévoreuse♀ de livres 111, 112 |
| bookstore | la librairie 8, 101, 103 |
| bookcase | la bibliothèque 75 |
| book | le livre 65, 111, 112 |
| body | le corps 68 |
| Blu-ray player | le lecteur Blu-ray 61 |
| blowjob, to give a | tailler une pipe ●※ 39 |
| blowjob | la pipe ●※ 39 |
| blouse | le chemisier 70, 71, 72 |
| blogger | le blogueur♂/la blogueuse♀ 55, 56 |
| blog, to | bloguer 55, 56 |
| bitch | la salope ●※ 113, 115, 117, 120, 121, 122, la pétasse ●※ 113, 115 |
| bisexual | bi 27, 28, 32 |
| bike | le vélo 83, 88, 89, 90 |
| best | meilleur♂/meilleure♀ 31, 33, 55, 96, 106 |
| belt | la ceinture 69, 70 |
| beer | la bière 95 |

| | |
|---|---|
| beep | le bip 63, 121 |
| bedroom | la chambre 74, 75, 76, 88, 89, 90 |
| bed | le lit 45, 74, 75, 76 |
| bear | l'ours♂ 31, 33 |
| beach | la plage 12, 13, 74, 85, 86 |
| battery | la batterie (in cell phone) 66, la pile (in radio) 60, 66 |
| bathing suit | le maillot de bain 68, 70, 72 |
| bar | le bar 31, 86, 88, 90, 95 |
| band | le groupe 54, 95, 104 |
| balls (body part) | les couilles ♀●※ 38, les burnes ♀●※ 38 |
| bag | le sac (as in paper or plastic) 81, 83, le sac à main (purse) 90 |
| bad | mal (adverb) 23, 49, 63, 79, 106, 107, 110, mauvais♂/mauvaise♀ (adjective) 76 |
| backpacking, to go | faire une randonnée 85, 86 |